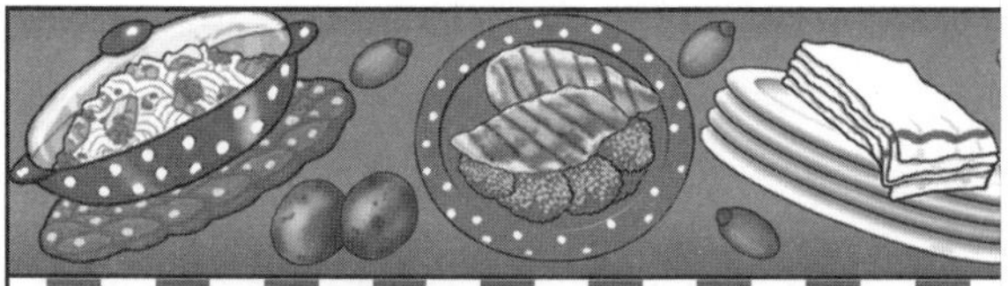

365 Easy Chicken Recipes

Quick, easy ways to cook chicken

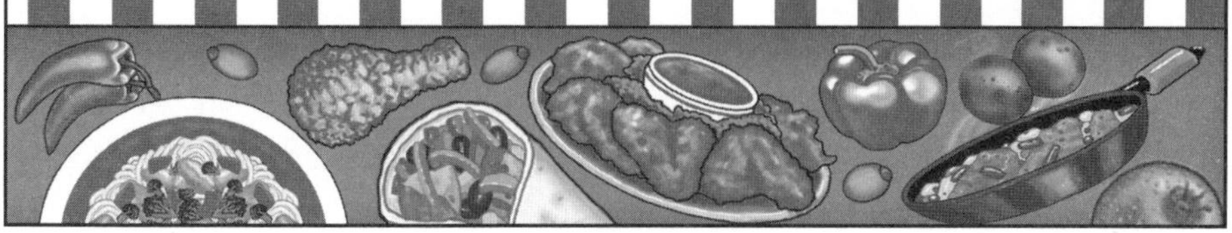

HB
HINKLER BOOKS

Cover by Nancy Bohanan
Pre-press by Graphic Print Group

365 Easy Chicken Recipes
Published in 2009 by Hinkler Books Pty Ltd
45–55 Fairchild Street
Heatherton VIC 3202 Australia
www.hinklerbooks.com

10 9 8 7 6 5 4 3 2
14 13 12 11 10

ISBN: 978 1 7418 3134 4
Printed and bound in China

Introduction

Welcome to the world of chicken – where the bird is king and the possibilities are endless. From a succulent roasted chicken to a classic chicken casserole, chicken has become a must-have kitchen staple with wonderful versatility. You can fry it, barbecue it, roast it, sauté it or find it rotisserie or deli-style in your local supermarket. Whether you're counting calories, carbohydrates, fat grams, your hard-earned money or your blessings, chicken is perfect 365 days a year because it's a simple, economical choice for healthy, hearty meals.

We bring you the ultimate chicken cookbook to give you a bird's eye view of the variety of ways to bring chicken to the table, with numerous time-saving dishes perfect for a quick dinner for the family after a hectic day or a dinner party for family and friends. This book strives to give you more of what you want – tasty and delectable chicken recipes that will save you time and effort, and make your life simpler and more enjoyable.

From fried chicken to wraps to exciting grilling ideas, ***365 Easy Chicken Recipes*** proves there's no limit to the delicious ways to cook the bird. Try **Chicken-Tortilla Dumplings**, a fun twist on traditional chicken and dumplings. Or how about serving up a fried dish with **Crunchy Chip Chicken**? **Dad's Best Smoked Chicken** is also an excellent choice, with its delicious lemonade marinade with a kick. Many of our recipes have that special something like a great technique or a knockout sauce. If you love chicken as we do, you will now have 365 more reasons to crave leftovers.

Cooking is one of life's simple pleasures. And these recipes make it easy to enjoy quality time with people you care about.

Contents

Introduction 3

Chicken: The Early Days 6

Bone up on your chicken history. Chickens have come a long way since they were depicted in Babylonian carvings in 600 BC and were believed to have special powers.

Dedication 7

Wings 'n' Things 9

Quick, beak-watering chicken starters ranging from imaginative finger food to hearty soups that will have your guests crowing for more.

Beak-Pleasing Casseroles 35

Please your flock with these simple, innovative chicken casseroles that are anything but ordinary. Each one is unique with its own distinct flavour and colourful combination of vegetables, cheeses and pastas. And all of them taste great!

Contents

Barnyard Bakes and Grills 117

From hearty to light, spicy to mild, these inventive chicken specialties will make you fly over the coop. Just combine these wonderful ingredients, put them in the oven – and stand back!

Birds of a Feather: Frys, Grills and Sautés 199

Make your brood happy in a snap with these quick and easy chicken sautés and frys. Grilling doesn't get any easier!

Slow Clucker 249

Pluck a little oregano here, stir in some veggies there, throw in some chicken and let your slow cooker do all the work! Over 60 savoury chicken recipes allow you to add ingredients to the cooker, go about your busy day and come home to a warm, wonderful dinner sure to please your flock.

One Last Peep 295

Ingredient Equivalents 296

Convenience Foods to Keep on Hand 300

Index 301

Chicken: The Early Days

The chicken is believed to have originated at least 4000 years ago in Asia, a region where some of the world's finest chicken recipes come from. There is evidence that centuries ago, people realised the value of chicken and raised chickens to provide meat and eggs as well. For example, chickens are depicted in Babylonian carvings as far back as 600 BCE and mentioned by early Greek writers, such as the playwright Aristophanes in 400 BCE. Indeed, the Romans considered chickens valuable and even sacred to Mars, the God of War.

In ancient Rome, people believed chickens had special powers and used them to predict the future. They also had a great number of recipes that involved chicken and eggs. Romans had several breeds of chickens and ate every part of the chicken, including the livers, gizzards and stomach.

Dedication

With a mission of helping you bring family and friends to the table, this book aims to make family meals and cooking for friends simple, easy and delicious.

We recognise the importance of a meal together as a means of building family bonds with memories and traditions that will be treasured for a lifetime. It is an opportunity to sit down with each other and share more than food.

This cookbook is dedicated with gratitude and respect to all those who show their love with homecooked meals, bringing family and friends to the table.

More and more statistical studies are finding that family meals play a significant role in childhood development. Children who eat with their families four or more nights per week are healthier, attain higher marks at school, score higher on aptitude tests and are less likely to have problems with drugs.

Wings 'n' Things

Quick, beak-watering chicken starters ranging from imaginative finger food to hearty soups that will have your guests crowing for more.

Wings 'n' Things Contents

Chilli-Honeyed Wings

18–20 wing drummettes and wing portions
1 cup (120 g) flour
¼ cup (60 g) butter
⅔ cup (230 g) honey
⅔ cup (180 g) chilli sauce
2 teaspoons minced garlic

- Preheat oven to 160° C (325° F).
- Press each wing in flour mixed with a little salt and cover well.
- Melt butter in large frypan. Brown chicken wings over medium-high heat and place in sprayed 23 x 33-cm (9 x 13-inch) glass baking dish.
- Combine honey, chilli sauce and garlic in small bowl and stir well.
- Spoon honey mixture over each wing and make sure some of sauce covers each wing.
- Cover and bake for 1 hour. Makes 18 to 20 wings.

Flautas de Pollo

Traditional flautas are filled with beef, chicken or pork and work as a main course, appetiser or side dish.

1 cup (140 g) cooked, minced chicken
12 flour tortillas
Canola oil
Guacamole
Salsa

- Spoon 1 rounded tablespoon (15 ml) chicken into the centre of each tortilla and roll into tight tube. Heat about 2 cm (1 inch) oil to about 175° C (350° F) in 4-L (4-quart) roasting pan or large, heavy frypan.
- Fry flautas in oil, turn once to brown on both sides and drain.
- Serve with choice of guacamole or salsa. Makes 12 flautas.

Deluxe Dinner Nachos

1 400-g (14-ounce) packet corn chips
230 g (8 ounces) shredded processed cheese
1 230-g (8-ounce) jar chopped jalapenos
1 300-g (11-ounce) can corn with liquid
1 425-g (15-ounce) can borlotti beans
2 cups (280 g) skinned, chopped roast chicken
Jalapeno chillies, chopped (to taste)
1 bunch spring onions, chopped
Salsa

- Preheat oven to 200° C (400° F).
- Place about three-quarters of corn chips in sprayed baking dish. Sprinkle half cheese and about 3 jalapenos on top. Heat just until cheese melts.
- Combine corn, beans, chicken and jalapeno chillies in saucepan. Heat over medium heat, stirring constantly, until mixture is hot. Spoon mixture over nachos, place dish in oven and heat for about 10 minutes.
- Sprinkle remaining cheese and spring onions over top and serve immediately. Garnish with remaining jalapeno chillies, remaining corn chips and salsa. Serves 8.

Chimichangas con Pollo

Chimichangas are deep-fried stuffed tortillas. Tucson, Arizona claims to be the birthplace of the chimichanga or chimi.

4–6 boneless, skinless chicken breast halves, cooked and shredded
3–4 fresh green chillies, roasted, peeled, chopped
2 tomatoes, peeled, seeded, chopped
1 onion, chopped finely
6–8 flour tortillas
Shredded cheddar cheese
120 g (4 ounces) shredded mozzarella cheese
Red or green chilli sauce

- Combine chicken, green chillies, tomatoes and onion and stir well to mix. Divide mixture evenly onto tortillas and top with cheeses. Fold ends like an envelope, roll and secure with toothpick.
- Place in deep fryer with oil heated to 175° C (350° F) and fry until golden brown. Drain and serve with chilli sauce. Serves 4.

When choosing a package of fresh chicken breasts, look for one that isn't too 'juicy'. Water is a sure sign of thawing. Look for medium-size, uniform breasts that will cook in the same amount of time.

Turkey Jerky

One of the best things in Texas is turkey jerky and it is found in many local supermarkets. Make your own Texan-style jerky with this easy recipe.

Turkey breasts, cooked

- Preheat oven to 80° C (175° F).
- Slice turkey breasts across the grain in very thin slices about 6 mm (¼ inch) thick.
- Place on baking tray and sprinkle both sides lightly with salt and a lot of freshly ground black pepper.
- Cook in oven until turkey gets to the right consistency. It should be very dense, dark brown, but not burned. (The time differs with the size of the pieces. Beef jerky takes 6 to 8 hours or more, but turkey jerky usually takes less time. Adjust time according to taste.) Serves 3 to 4.

Easy Crispy Chicken Tacos

Everybody goes for this classic. Crispy taco shells with chicken, beef or fish make great treats.

8–10 taco shells, warmed
4–6 boneless, skinless chicken breast halves, cooked, chopped
1 cup (250 g) diced tomato, drained
½ cup (110 g) diced onion
1 cup (80 g) chopped lettuce
340 g (12 ounces) shredded cheddar cheese
1 230-g (8-ounce) jar spicy salsa

- Make tacos by filling each taco shell with chicken, tomato, onion, lettuce and cheese. Serve with salsa. Serves 4 to 6.

Chicken for Lunch

4 cooked, thick chicken breast slices from deli
85 g (3 ounces) cream cheese, softened
3 tablespoons (40 g) salsa
2 tablespoons (30 g) mayonnaise

- Place chicken on serving platter.
- Beat cream cheese, salsa and mayonnaise in bowl until smooth and creamy.
- Place 1 heaped tablespoon (15 ml) cream cheese mixture on top of each chicken slice and serve cold. Serves 4.

Cracked-Pepper Turkey Breast

This is a delicious turkey breast that can be served many ways. Leftovers are great in turkey sandwiches and turkey casserole.

1 1.1–1.4 kg (2½–3 pound) refrigerated cooked turkey breast
Cracked pepper (to taste)
1 455-g (16-ounce) jar hot salsa
230 g (8 ounces) shredded cheese

- Slice enough turkey for each person and sprinkle with cracked pepper. Spoon 1 heaped tablespoon (15 ml) salsa over each slice and sprinkle a little cheese over top. Serves 6.

Chicken Kiev with Honey-Ginger Glaze

Canola oil
450 g (1 pound) frozen, pre-cooked chicken kievs
Rice, cooked
⅔ cup (230 g) honey
2 teaspoons peeled, grated fresh ginger
1 tablespoon (15 ml) Worcestershire sauce
1 tablespoon (15 ml) soy sauce
1 tablespoon (15 ml) lemon juice

- Place a little oil in heavy frypan and cook chicken kievs for about 5 minutes on each side or until they brown.
- Combine honey, ginger, white wine, Worcestershire sauce, soy sauce and lemon juice into a bowl, mix well and pour into frypan. Bring mixture to a boil, reduce heat and simmer for 15 minutes. Serve over rice. Serves 4.

Avoid cross-contamination of utensils used on raw poultry and avoid packages that leak.

TIP: *You might want to try the new type of rice that can be microwaved for 90 seconds – and it's ready to serve.*

Chicken-Noodle Soup

1 85-g (3-ounce) packet chicken-flavoured ramen noodles, broken
280 g (10 ounces) frozen green peas, thawed
1 115-g (4-ounce) tin sliced mushrooms, drained
3 cups (450 g) cooked, cubed chicken

- Heat 2¼ cups (560 ml) water in large saucepan to boiling. Add noodles, contents of seasoning packet and peas. Heat to boiling, then reduce heat to medium and cook for about 5 minutes.
- Stir in mushrooms and chicken and continue cooking over low heat until all ingredients are hot. To serve, spoon into soup bowls. Serves 6.

Five-Can Soup Bowl

400 ml (14 ounces) chicken stock
1 280-g (10-ounce) can cream of chicken soup
340 g (12 ounces) cooked chicken breast
1 425-g (15-ounce) can Mexican beans
1 280-g (10-ounce) can tomatoes
Green chillies, sliced (to taste)
Corn chips, crushed coarsely
Shredded cheese
Sour cream

- Combine stock, soup, chicken, beans, tomatoes and green chillies in saucepan and simmer for 30 minutes. Serve over corn chips and top with cheese and sour cream. Serves 6.

Northern Chilli

2 onions, coarsely chopped
Olive oil
3 425-g (15-ounce) cans cannellini beans, drained
800 ml (28 ounces) chicken stock
2 tablespoons (25 g) minced garlic
1 200-g (7-ounce) jar chopped green chillies
1 tablespoon (15 g) ground cumin
3 cups (420 g) cooked, finely chopped chicken breasts
230 g (8 ounces) shredded cheddar cheese

- Cook onions with a little oil in large, heavy pot for about 5 minutes, but do not brown.
- Place 1 can beans in shallow bowl and mash with fork. Combine mashed beans, 2 remaining cans of beans, chicken stock, garlic, green chillies and cumin in saucepan. Bring to a boil and reduce heat.
- Cover and simmer for 30 minutes. Add chopped chicken, stir to blend well and heat until chilli is thoroughly hot. When serving, top each bowl with 3 tablespoons (20 g) cheese. Serves 6.

Q: What do you get if you cross a chicken with a cement mixer?

A: A bricklayer.

Chicken and Vegetable Stew Pot

200 g (7 ounces) onions, chopped
250 g (9 ounces) red and green capsicums, chopped
Olive oil
2 tablespoons (25 g) minced garlic
2 tablespoons (30 g) chilli powder
3 teaspoons ground cumin
900 g (2 pounds) cooked chicken tenderloin, cubed
800 ml (27 ounces) chicken stock
3 425-g (15-ounce) cans borlotti beans
Jalapeno chillies, sliced (to taste)

- Cook onions and capsicums with a little oil in a frypan for about 5 minutes, stirring occasionally. Add garlic, chilli powder, cumin and cubed chicken and cook an additional 5 minutes.
- Stir in stock and a little salt. Bring to a boil and reduce heat. Cover and simmer for 15 minutes.
- Place 1 can beans in shallow bowl and mash with fork. Add mashed beans, remaining 2 cans beans and chillies to pot. Bring to boil, reduce heat and simmer for 10 minutes. Serves 8.

Hearty 15-Minute Turkey Soup

400 ml (14 ounces) chicken stock
3 425-g (15-ounce) cans cannellini beans, rinsed and drained
1 800-g (28-ounce) can diced tomatoes with liquid
2–3 cups (280–420 g) small chunks cooked white turkey meat
2 teaspoons minced garlic
¼ teaspoon cayenne pepper
Freshly grated parmesan cheese for garnish

- Mix all ingredients except cheese in saucepan and heat. Garnish with parmesan cheese before serving. Serves 6.

Day-After-Christmas Turkey Chilli

1.4 kg (3 pounds) minced turkey
½ teaspoon garlic powder
3 tablespoons (45 g) chilli powder
1 230-g (8-ounce) jar tomato simmer sauce
Shredded cheese

- Combine turkey and garlic powder with 1 cup (250 ml) water in large saucepan. Cook over medium heat until mixture begins to fry.
- Add chilli powder and tomato sauce and simmer until meat is tender. Garnish with cheese. Serves 6.

Old-Fashioned Chicken and Dumplings

900 g (2 pounds) boneless, skinless chicken breasts
½ onion, chopped
½ cup (50 g) sliced celery
1 carrot, sliced
3 tablespoons (30 g) shortening
2 cups (240 g) flour

- Place chicken in large soup pot and cover with water.
- Add onion, celery, carrot, 1 teaspoon salt and ½ teaspoon pepper.
- Cover and cook for 40 minutes or until chicken is tender. Remove chicken and break into bite-sized pieces.
- Strain broth and return to pot.
- Cut shortening into flour and 1 teaspoon salt in large bowl with pastry blender or fork until dough is pea-sized. Add 9 tablespoons (135 ml) iced water one at a time and mix lightly with fork.
- On a floured surface, roll dough very thinly and keep rolling pin well floured. Cut into strips and layer on baking paper. Refrigerate for 45 minutes.
- Bring broth and chicken pieces to boil. Drop dough strips into boiling broth and chicken pieces. Do not stir, just jiggle or shake pot. (Stirring will break up the dumplings.) Cook on medium heat for 30 minutes. Serves 8.

Hot Gobble Gobble Soup

This is spicy, but not too much, just right!

3–4 cups (420–560 g) cooked chopped turkey
3 280-g (10-ounce) cans condensed chicken stock
2 280-g (10-ounce) cans diced tomatoes
Green chillies, sliced (to taste)
1 425-g (15-ounce) can corn, drained
1 large onion, chopped
1 280-g (10-ounce) can tomato soup
1 teaspoon garlic powder
1 teaspoon dried oregano
3 tablespoons (25 g) cornflour

- Combine turkey, stock, tomatoes, green chillies, corn, onion, tomato soup, garlic powder and oregano in large roasting pan.
- Mix cornflour with 3 tablespoons (45 ml) water and add to soup mixture. Bring to a boil, reduce heat and simmer, stirring occasionally, for about 2 hours. Serves 6.

Never partially cook poultry and store to finish later. The heat may simply start cultivating bacteria that will be thriving too strongly to be fully destroyed by the briefer cooking time when you finish cooking it.

White Lightning Chilli

1½ cups (400 g) dried cannellini beans
1.2 L (40 ounces) chicken stock
2 tablespoons (30 g) butter
1 onion, chopped
1 clove garlic, minced
3 cups (420 g) chopped, cooked chicken
1 115-g (4-ounce) jar chopped green chillies
½ teaspoon dried basil
1½ teaspoons ground cumin
½ teaspoon dried oregano
6 20-cm (8-inch) flour tortillas
Shredded cheddar cheese

- Wash beans and place in a large, heavy pan. Cover with water 5 cm (2 inches) above beans and soak overnight. Drain beans, add stock, butter, 1 cup (250 ml) water, onion and garlic and bring to boil. Reduce heat, cover and simmer for 2 hours 30 minutes. Stir occasionally.
- With a potato masher, mash half the beans. Add chicken, green chillies, basil, ½ teaspoon pepper, cumin and oregano. Bring to a boil, reduce heat, cover and simmer for an additional 30 minutes.
- With kitchen shears, make 4 cuts in each tortilla towards the centre, but not through the centre. Line serving bowls with tortillas and overlap cut edges. Spoon in chilli and top with cheese. Serves 6.

TIP: Some people like to add ⅛ teaspoon each of cayenne pepper and ground cloves.

Chicken Waldorf Salad

450 g (1 pound) boneless, skinless chicken breasts
1 red apple with peel, sliced
1 green apple with peel, sliced
1 cup (100 g) sliced celery
½ cup (65 g) chopped walnuts
2 170-g (6-ounce) tubs yoghurt
½ cup (110 g) mayonnaise
170 g (6 ounces) shredded lettuce
Thin slices of orange (to garnish)

- Place chicken in large saucepan and cover with water. Cook on high heat for about 15 minutes, drain and cool. Cut into 2.5-cm (1-inch) pieces, season with salt and pepper and place in large salad bowl.
- Add sliced apples, celery and walnuts. Stir in yoghurt and mayonnaise and toss to mix well. (May be served at room temperature or refrigerate for several hours.) Serve over shredded lettuce and decorate with orange slices. Serves 6.

A comb is the flesh on the top of a chicken's head.

Chicken Medley Supreme

1 cup (160 g) chopped onion
1 cup (100 g) chopped celery
Olive oil
170 g (6 ounces) long-grain and wild rice mix, cooked
1 280-g (10-ounce) can cream of chicken soup
1 115-g (4-ounce) jar chopped roasted red capsicum
1 425-g (15-ounce) can green beans, drained
½ cup (85 g) slivered almonds
1 cup (225 g) mayonnaise
3 cups (170 g) lightly crushed potato chips

- Preheat oven to 175° C (350° F).
- Sauté onion and celery with a little oil in frypan. Combine all ingredients in large bowl except potato chips. Season with a little salt and pepper.
- Spray 23 x 33-cm (9 x 13-inch) baking dish and spoon mixture into dish. Sprinkle crushed potato chips over casserole and bake for 35 minutes or until chips are light brown. Serves 8.

After-Christmas Salad

560 g (20 ounces) cos lettuce
2½–3 cups (350–420 g) cooked, sliced turkey
1 230-g (8-ounce) tin baby corn, quartered
2 tomatoes, chopped
230 g (8 ounces) shredded Colby cheese
⅔ cup (150 g) mayonnaise
⅔ cup (175 g) salsa
¼ cup (60 ml) cider vinegar
2 tablespoons (25 g) sugar

- Combine cos lettuce, turkey, baby corn, tomatoes and cheese in large salad bowl.
- Combine mayonnaise, salsa, vinegar and sugar into a bowl. When ready to serve sprinkle with a little salt and pepper, spoon dressing over salad and toss to coat well. Serves 4.

TIP: This is a wonderful salad just like this, but if you have some ripe olives, red onion, borlotti beans or precooked bacon, throw it in the bowl. It will be even better.

Pasta and Turkey Salad Supper

340 g (12 ounces) tri-colour spiral pasta
1 115-g (4-ounce) jar sliced black olives, drained
1 cup each (70 g/100 g) fresh broccoli and cauliflower florets
2 small yellow squash, sliced
1 cup (150 g) halved cherry tomatoes
1 230-g (8-ounce) bottle ranch dressing
680 g (1½ pounds) smoked turkey breast, sliced
Cracked pepper (to taste)

- Cook pasta according to package directions. Drain and rinse in cold water. Combine with olives, broccoli, cauliflower, sliced squash and tomatoes in large salad bowl.
- Toss with dressing. Place thin slices of turkey breast, arranged in rows, over salad and sprinkle with cracked pepper. Serve immediately. Serves 8.

Chickens and turkeys are known to cross-breed and are known as 'turkins'.

Cheesy Caesar Pizza

1 30-cm (12-inch) Italian pizza crust
230 g (8 ounces) shredded mozzarella cheese
170 g (6 ounces) cooked chicken breast strips
2 cups (150 g) shredded lettuce
3 spring onions, sliced
¾ cup (85 g) shredded cheddar-Colby cheese
½ 230-g (8-ounce) bottle caesar dressing

- Preheat oven to 205° C (400° F).
- Top pizza crust with mozzarella cheese and bake for 8 minutes or until cheese melts.
- Combine chicken strips, lettuce, spring onions and cheese in bowl. Pour about half of caesar dressing over salad and toss.
- Top hot pizza with salad and cut into wedges. Serve immediately. Serves 4.

Q: Why did the chicken cross the road?

A: To prove to the armadillo that it could be done.

Raisin and Rice Chicken Salad

3 cups (285 g) instant brown rice
¼ cup (60 g) butter
3 cups (420 g) finely chopped cooked chicken breasts
½ cup (75 g) sultanas
½ cup (75 g) chopped red capsicum
2 tablespoons (30 ml) lemon juice
1 tablespoon (15 ml) Dijon-style mustard
2 tablespoons (45 g) honey
1 teaspoon white wine vinegar
¼ cup (40 g) slivered almonds, toasted

- Cook brown rice according to package directions. Add butter and a little salt and pepper. While rice is still hot, stir in chopped chicken, sultanas and capsicum. Transfer to serving bowl.
- Combine lemon juice, mustard, honey and wine vinegar in jar and shake until ingredients blend well. Drizzle over rice-chicken mixture and sprinkle with almonds. Serves 4.

TIP: Toasting brings out the flavours of nuts and seeds. Place nuts or seeds on baking tray and bake at 110° C (225° F) for 10 minutes. Be careful not to burn them.

Bridge Club Luncheon Chicken

1 rotisserie-cooked chicken
1 cup (150 g) red or green grapes, halved
2 cups (200 g) chopped celery
⅔ cup (90 g) whole walnuts
⅔ cup (110 g) sliced spring onion
½ cup (110 g) mayonnaise
1 tablespoon (15 ml) orange juice
2 tablespoons (30 ml) red wine vinegar
1 teaspoon chilli powder
1 teaspoon paprika

- Skin chicken, cut chicken breast into thin strips and place in bowl with lid. (Reserve dark meat for another use.) Add red or green grapes, celery, walnuts and sliced onions.
- Combine mayonnaise, orange juice, vinegar, chilli powder and paprika in a bowl, add a little salt and pepper and mix well. Spoon over salad mixture and toss. Serves 8.

Q: What do you get when you cross a chicken and a pit bull?

A: Just the pit bull.

Luscious Pawpaw and Chicken Salad

280 g (10 ounces) cos lettuce, torn
2 ripe pawpaws, peeled, seeded and cubed
1 large red capsicum, seeded and sliced
2 cups (280 g) cooked, cubed chicken breasts
⅓ cup (40 g) pecan pieces, toasted
¼ cup (60 ml) lime juice
¼ cup (85 g) honey
2 teaspoons minced garlic
1 teaspoon Dijon-style mustard
3 tablespoons (45 ml) extra-virgin olive oil

- Combine lettuce, pawpaws and capsicum in large salad bowl. Whisk lime juice, honey, garlic, mustard and a little salt in small bowl. Slowly add olive oil in thin stream and whisk dressing until it blends well.
- Pour lime juice, honey, garlic, mustard and olive oil over salad, add cubed chicken and toss. To serve, sprinkle pecans over top of salad. Serves 6.

Chicken and Rice Salad Supreme

300 g (10 ounces) cooked chicken breast
2 250-g (9-ounce) pouches brown microwave rice
⅔ cup (35 g) sun-dried tomatoes
2 ripe avocados, peeled and diced
¾ cup (190 g) Dijon-style mustard vinaigrette dressing

- Chop chicken into chunks. Prepare microwave rice according to package directions.
- Combine chicken, rice, tomatoes and avocado in bowl.
- In separate bowl, combine vinaigrette dressing and ½ teaspoon salt. Gently stir into chicken-rice mixture and refrigerate for 2 hours before serving. Serves 8.

Q: Why did the chewing gum cross the road?

A: It was stuck to the foot of a chicken.

Chinese Chicken Salad

2 cups (280 g) cooked, chopped chicken
1 cup (100 g) diced celery
300 g (11 ounces) mandarin segments
⅓ cup (65 g) sliced almonds, toasted
¾ cup (55 g) whipped cream
¾ cup (175 ml) Thousand Island dressing
1 cup (55 g) chow mein noodles

- Mix chicken, celery, mandarins and almonds in large bowl.
- In separate bowl, mix whipped cream, dressing, noodles and ½ teaspoon salt.
- Combine dressing with salad and serve immediately. Serves 6.

TIP: You can make the salad in advance, but mix the dressing right before serving.

Barbecued Chicken Salad

3 boneless, skinless chicken breasts, grilled
255 g (9 ounces) cos lettuce, torn
1 425-g (15-ounce) can black beans or borlotti beans, rinsed, drained
12–15 cherry tomatoes
¾ cup (175 ml) ranch dressing
3 tablespoons (45 g) barbecue sauce
2 tablespoons (35 g) salsa

- Cut chicken in strips and heat. Place chicken strips, lettuce, beans and cherry tomatoes in bowl and toss with enough dressing to lightly coat.
- Combine ranch dressing, barbecue sauce and salsa in bowl and refrigerate. Serves 6 to 8.

Strawberry and Chicken Salad

450 g (1 pound) boneless, skinless chicken breast halves
Olive oil
280 g (10 ounces) mixed spring greens
450 g (1 pint) fresh strawberries, sliced
½ cup (65 g) chopped walnuts
¾ cup (255 g) honey
⅔ cup (165 ml) red wine vinegar
1 tablespoon (15 ml) soy sauce
½ teaspoon ground ginger

- Cut chicken into strips and place in large frypan with a little oil. Cook and stir on medium-high heat for about 10 minutes.
- While chicken cooks, combine honey, vinegar, soy sauce and ginger into a bowl and mix well. After chicken strips cook, pour ½ cup (125 ml) dressing into frypan with chicken and cook additional 2 minutes or until liquid evaporates.
- Combine spring greens, strawberries and walnuts in salad bowl. Pour in remaining dressing and toss. Top with chicken strips. Serves 6.

Q: Why was the chicken afraid of the chicken?

A: Because he was chicken.

Beak-Pleasing Casseroles

Please your flock with these simple, innovative chicken casseroles that are anything but ordinary. Each one is unique with its own distinct flavour and colourful combination of vegetables, cheeses and pastas. And all of them taste great!

Beak-Pleasing Casseroles Contents

Beak-Pleasing Casseroles Contents

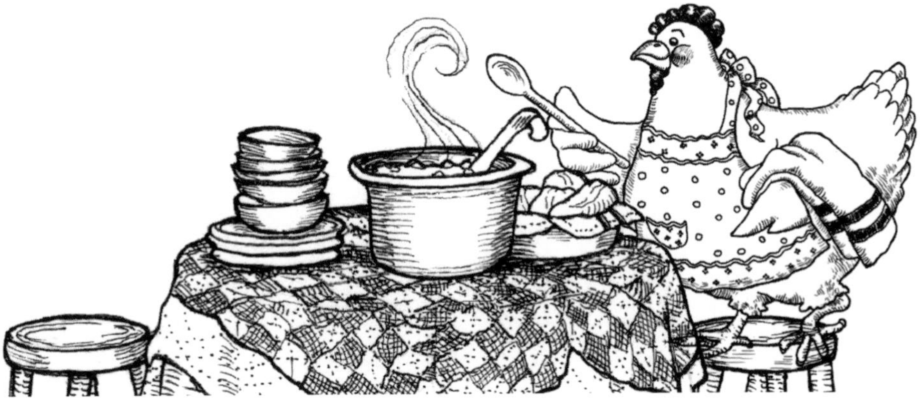

Three-Cheese Turkey Casserole

1 230-g (8-ounce) packet fettuccini (egg noodles)
1 teaspoon olive oil
3 tablespoons (45 g) butter
¾ cup (110 g) chopped green capsicum
½ cup (50 g) chopped celery
½ cup (80 g) chopped onion
1 280-g (10-ounce) can cream of chicken soup
½ cup (125 ml) milk
1 170-g (6-ounce) tin whole mushrooms
450 g (16 ounces) cottage cheese
4 cups (560 g) diced cooked turkey or chicken
340 g (12 ounces) shredded cheddar cheese
¾ cup (75 g) freshly grated parmesan cheese

- Preheat oven to 175° C (350° F).
- Place pasta in 3 L (3 quarts) hot water, add 1 tablespoon (15 ml) salt and oil in large soup pot and cook according to package directions.
- Melt butter in frypan and sauté capsicum, celery and onion.
- Combine pasta, capsicum-onion mixture, chicken soup, milk, mushrooms, ½ teaspoon pepper, cottage cheese, turkey and cheddar cheese in large bowl.
- Pour into sprayed 23 x 33-cm (9 x 13-inch) baking dish and top with parmesan cheese. Bake for 40 minutes. Serves 10.

Clucky Clucky Casserole

450 g (16 ounces) broccoli florets
3 cups (420 g) cooked, diced chicken
1 280-g (10-ounce) can cream of chicken soup
2 tablespoons (30 ml) milk
⅓ cup (75 g) mayonnaise
2 teaspoons lemon juice
3 tablespoons (45 g) butter, melted
1 cup (60 g) breadcrumbs or cracker crumbs
⅓ cup (40 g) shredded cheddar cheese

- Preheat oven to 175° C (350° F).
- Cook broccoli until tender and drain.
- Place broccoli in sprayed 23 x 33-cm (9 x 13-inch) glass baking dish. Sprinkle 1 teaspoon salt over broccoli and cover with diced chicken.
- Combine soup, milk, mayonnaise, lemon juice and ¼ teaspoon pepper in saucepan. Heat just enough to dilute soup a little and pour over chicken.
- Mix melted butter, breadcrumbs and cheese in bowl and sprinkle over soup mixture. Bake for 30 minutes or until mixture is hot and bubbly. Serves 8.

Easy Chicken Enchiladas

10 corn tortillas
1 280-g (10-ounce) can mushroom soup
1 280-g (10-ounce) can cream of chicken soup
1 cup (250 ml) milk
1 small onion, chopped
400 g (14 ounces) chilli salsa
4–5 boneless, skinless chicken breast halves, cooked
340 g (12 ounces) shredded cheddar cheese

- Preheat oven to 175° C (350° F).
- Cut tortillas into 2-cm (1-inch) strips and lay half of them in sprayed 23 x 33-cm (9 x 13-inch) baking dish.
- Mix mushroom soup, chicken soup, milk, onion and salsa in saucepan and heat just enough to mix.
- Chop cooked chicken and place half on top of tortilla strips in baking dish. Pour half of sauce on top of chicken, then repeat tortilla layer and sauce layer.
- Cover and bake for 45 minutes. Uncover, sprinkle with cheese and bake for an additional 10 minutes. Serve hot. Serves 8.

Q: How do chickens bake a cake?

A: From scratch.

Busy Day Chicken Casserole

6 boneless, skinless chicken breast halves, cooked
450 g (1 pint) sour cream
200 g (7 ounces) spaghetti
2 280-g (10-ounce) cans cream of chicken soup
1 115-g (4-ounce) can mushrooms, drained
½ cup (115 g) butter, melted
1 cup (100 g) fresh grated parmesan cheese

- Preheat oven to 175° C (350° F).
- Cut chicken into strips and combine all ingredients, except parmesan cheese, with ⅛ teaspoon pepper in bowl and mix well.
- Pour into sprayed 23 x 33-cm (9 x 13-inch) baking dish and sprinkle cheese on top. Bake covered for 50 minutes. Serves 6.

Hot-n-Sour Chicky Casserole

1 85-g (3-ounce) package chicken-flavoured instant ramen noodles
1 455-g (16-ounce) package frozen broccoli, cauliflower and carrots
⅔ cup (180 g) sweet-and-sour sauce
3 boneless, skinless chicken breast halves, cooked

- Cook noodles and vegetables in 2 cups (500 ml) boiling water in saucepan for 3 minutes, stir occasionally and drain.
- Add contents of seasoning packet, sweet-and-sour sauce and a little salt and pepper to noodle mixture.
- Cut chicken into strips, add chicken to noodle mixture and heat thoroughly. Serves 6.

Turkey and Broccoli Bake

450 g (16 ounces) broccoli florets
2 cups (280 g) cooked, diced leftover turkey or chicken
1 280-g (10-ounce) can cream of chicken soup
½ cup (110 g) mayonnaise
2 tablespoons (30 ml) lemon juice
⅓ cup (35 g) grated parmesan cheese

- Preheat oven to 175° C (350° F).
- Arrange broccoli florets in sprayed 23 x 33-cm (9 x 13-inch) baking dish and sprinkle with diced turkey.
- Combine chicken soup, mayonnaise, lemon juice, cheese and ¼ cup (60 ml) water in saucepan. Heat just enough to mix well.
- Spoon over broccoli and turkey. Cover and bake for 20 minutes, uncover and continue baking for an additional 15 minutes. Serves 6 to 8.

The term 'cull' refers to removing a bird from the flock because of productivity, age, health or personality issues.

Chicken-Tortilla Dumplings

This is a great recipe and using tortillas is a lot easier than making real dumplings!

6 large boneless, skinless chicken breast halves, cubed
2 sticks celery, chopped
1 onion, chopped
2 tablespoons (20 g) chicken stock powder
1 280-g (10-ounce) can cream of chicken soup
10 20-cm (8-inch) flour tortillas

- Place chicken, 10 cups (2.25 L) water, celery and onion in roasting pan.
- Bring to a boil, reduce heat and cook about 30 minutes or until chicken is tender. Remove chicken and set aside to cool.
- Save broth in roasting pan (about 9 cups/2 L broth). Add chicken stock powder and taste to make sure it is rich and tasty. (Add more stock powder if needed and more water if you don't have 9 cups/2 L broth.) Add chicken soup to broth and bring to boil.
- Cut tortillas into 5-cm x 2.5-cm (2-inch x 1-inch) strips. Add strips, one at a time, to briskly boiling broth mixture and stir constantly.
- When all strips are in saucepan, pour in chicken broth, reduce heat to low and simmer for 5 to 10 minutes. Stir well but gently to prevent dumplings from sticking. (The pot of chicken and dumplings will be very thick.)
- Pour into very large serving bowl and serve hot. Serves 10.

Rule-the-Roost Casserole

100 g (3½ ounces) chicken-flavored rice
100 g (3½ ounces) macaroni
1 280-g (10-ounce) can cream of mushroom soup
1 280-g (10-ounce) can cream of celery soup
3 cups (420 g) cooked, chopped chicken or turkey
280 g (10 ounces) frozen peas, thawed
1 cup (115 g) shredded cheddar cheese

- Preheat oven to 175° C (350° F).
- Cook rice and macaroni according to package directions. Mix both soups with ½ cup (125 ml) water.
- Combine chicken, cooked rice and macaroni, soups, peas and cheese in bowl and mix well.
- Pour into sprayed 3-L (3-quart) baking dish and bake covered for 40 minutes. Serves 6.

Cheesy Chick Bake

8 boneless, skinless chicken breast halves
8 slices Swiss cheese
1 280-g (10-ounce) can cream of chicken soup
1 230-g (8-ounce) box chicken stuffing mix

- Preheat oven to 160° C (325° F).
- Flatten each chicken breast with rolling pin and place in sprayed 23 x 33-cm (9 x 13-inch) baking dish.
- Place cheese slices over chicken.
- Combine chicken soup and ½ cup (125 ml) water and pour over chicken.
- Prepare stuffing mix according to package directions and sprinkle over chicken.
- Bake for 1 hour. Serves 8.

Chicken Breasts Supreme

6 boneless, skinless chicken breast halves
¼ cup (60 g) butter
1 280-g (10-ounce) can cream of chicken soup
¾ cup (175 ml) white wine or chicken stock
1 240-g (8½-ounce) can sliced water chestnuts, drained
1 115-g (4-ounce) jar sliced mushrooms, drained
2 tablespoons (20 g) chopped green capsicums
¼ teaspoon crushed thyme leaves

- Preheat oven to 175° C (350° F).
- Brown chicken in butter on all sides in frypan. Arrange in 23 x 33-cm (9 x 13-inch) baking pan. Sprinkle with ½ teaspoon salt and dash of pepper.
- Add soup to butter that is left in frypan and slowly stir in wine or stock. Add remaining ingredients and heat to boil.
- Pour soup mixture over chicken. Cover and bake for 45 minutes. Remove cover and bake for an additional 15 minutes. Serves 6.

If a rooster is not present in a flock of hens, a hen will often take the role, stop laying and begin to crow.

Chicken Chow Mein

3½ cups (490 g) cooked, cubed chicken breasts
2 280-g (10-ounce) cans cream of chicken soup
800 g (28 ounces) frozen stir-fry vegetables, thawed
1 230-g (8-ounce) can sliced water chestnuts, drained
¾ cup (105 g) chopped cashew nuts
1 green capsicum, seeded and chopped
1 onion, chopped
1 cup (100 g) chopped celery
¼ teaspoon chilli sauce
1¼ cups (70 g) chow mein noodles

- Preheat oven to 175° C (350° F).
- Combine chicken, soup, vegetables, water chestnuts, cashew nuts, capsicum, onion, celery and chilli sauce in large bowl. Stir to mix well.
- Spoon into sprayed 23 x 33-cm (9 x 13-inch) baking dish. Sprinkle noodles over top of casserole.
- Bake for 35 minutes or until it bubbles at edges of casserole. Let stand for 5 minutes before serving. Serves 8.

Chicken Dish, WOW!

1 280-g (10-ounce) can cream of chicken soup
1 280-g (10-ounce) can spicy tomato soup
1 145-g (5-ounce) can evaporated milk
2 425-g (15-ounce) cans green beans, drained
1 teaspoon chicken stock powder
4 cups (560 g) cooked, cubed chicken breasts
1 red capsicum, chopped
2 sticks celery, sliced
¼ cup (40 g) chopped onion
1 cup (55 g) chow mein noodles
½ cup (85 g) slivered almonds
85 g (3 ounces) onion, finely chopped and fried until crispy

- Preheat oven to 175° C (350° F).
- Combine chicken soup, tomato soup and evaporated milk in bowl and mix well.
- Fold in green beans, chicken stock, chicken, capsicum, celery, onion, noodles, almonds, and ½ teaspoon each of salt and pepper.
- Spoon into sprayed 23 x 33-cm (9 x 13-inch) baking dish.
- Bake covered for 35 minutes. Remove from oven and sprinkle onion over casserole.
- Place back in oven and bake for an additional 10 minutes. Serves 12.

TIP: This casserole may easily be made ahead of time and baked the next day. Just wait to add the onion until you put it in the oven.

Chicken Divan

560 g (20 ounces) frozen broccoli
4–6 boneless, skinless chicken breast halves, cooked, sliced
2 280-g (10-ounce) cans cream of chicken soup
1 cup (225 g) mayonnaise
1 teaspoon lemon juice
½ teaspoon curry powder or Worcestershire sauce
1½ cups (170 g) shredded sharp cheese, divided
½ cup (60 g) seasoned breadcrumbs
1 teaspoon butter, melted

- Preheat oven to 175° C (350° F).
- Cook broccoli in saucepan until tender and drain. Arrange broccoli in sprayed 23 x 33-cm (9 x 13-inch) baking dish. Place chicken slices on top.
- Combine soup, mayonnaise, lemon juice, curry and ¾ cup (85 g) cheese in bowl and spread over chicken.
- In separate bowl, combine breadcrumbs and butter and layer over chicken. Sprinkle remaining cheese over top and bake for 25 to 30 minutes. Serves 8.

A boneless chicken breast will cook in less than 10 minutes in a steamer. After you remove the chicken, let it sit uncut for 2 to 3 minutes, and any slight pinkness on the interior will gently finish cooking in the chicken's own steam.

Chicken Spaghetti

3 boneless, skinless chicken breasts, boiled
1 280-g (10-ounce) can tomatoes
Green chillies (to taste)
1 280-g (10-ounce) can cream of mushroom soup
230 g (8 ounces) shredded cheddar cheese
230 g (8 ounces) shredded processed cheese
340 g (12 ounces) spaghetti

- Preheat oven to 175° C (350° F).
- Shred cooked chicken into large bowl. Add tomatoes, green chillies, soup, cheddar cheese and processed cheese. Boil spaghetti according to package directions and drain.
- Add to chicken mixture and mix well. Pour into a 3-litre (3-quart) baking dish. Cover and bake for 35 minutes. Serves 8.

Curried Chicken Casserole

1 280-g (10-ounce) packet chicken-flavoured rice
1 teaspoon curry powder
300 g (11 ounces) cooked chicken, chopped
¾ cup (175 ml) chicken stock
⅓ cup (50 g) raisins, optional

- Preheat oven to 175° C (350° F).
- Prepare rice according to package directions.
- Add curry powder, chicken, chicken stock and raisins and mix well.
- Pour into sprayed 18 x 28-cm (7 x 11-inch) baking pan. Cover and bake for 15 minutes. Serves 6.

Manuel's Fiesta Chicken

½ cup (115 g) butter
5–6 boneless, skinless chicken breast halves
2 cups (120 g) finely crushed cheese crackers
2 tablespoons (30 g) taco seasoning mix
1 bunch spring onions with tops, chopped
1 teaspoon chicken stock powder
500 ml (1 pint) whipping cream
230 g (8 ounces) shredded cheese
1 115-g (4-ounce) can chopped green chillies, drained

- Preheat oven to 175° C (350° F).
- Melt butter in 23 x 33-cm (9 x 13-inch) baking dish and set aside.
- Pound chicken breasts to ½ cm (¼ inch) thick. Combine cracker crumbs and taco seasoning in bowl and mix well. Dredge chicken in mixture and make sure crumbs stick to chicken.
- Place chicken breasts in baking dish with butter. Remove several tablespoons melted butter from dish and place in saucepan. Add onions and sauté. Reduce heat and add chicken stock powder.
- Stir well and add whipping cream, cheese and green chillies. Pour mixture over chicken in baking dish and bake for 55 minutes. Serves 8.

Chicken Martinez

1 280-g (10-ounce) can spicy tomato soup
1 280-g (10-ounce) can cream of chicken soup
1 230-g (8-ounce) tub sour cream
1 onion, chopped
1 280-g (10-ounce) can diced tomatoes
Green chillies, chopped (to taste)
1 425-g (15-ounce) can kidney beans, rinsed and drained
1 425-g (15-ounce) can corn, drained
1 teaspoon chilli powder
1 tablespoon (15 g) taco seasoning
8 flour tortillas, cut into strips
4–5 large boneless, skinless chicken breast halves, cooked, cut into strips
120 g (4 ounces) shredded mozzarella cheese
120 g (4 ounces) shredded cheddar cheese

- Preheat oven to 175° C (350° F).
- Combine soups, sour cream, onion, tomatoes, green chillies, beans, corn, chilli powder and taco seasoning in large bowl and mix well.
- Spread small amount of soup-bean mixture into sprayed 23 x 33-cm (9 x 13-inch) baking dish.
- Arrange half of tortilla strips over soup-bean mixture. Make 1 layer of chicken, another layer of half soup-bean mixture, remaining tortilla strips and remaining chicken. Top with remaining soup-bean mixture.
- Cover and bake for 45 minutes or until it bubbles.
- Uncover and spread shredded cheese over top of casserole. Return to oven for about 5 minutes until cheese melts. Serves 10.

Classic Chicken Marsala

5–6 boneless, skinless chicken breast halves
3 eggs, beaten
4 tablespoons (60 ml) oil
Italian seasoned breadcrumbs
450 g (1 pound) fresh mushrooms, sliced
2–3 cloves garlic, minced
1 280-g (10-ounce) packet chicken stock
½ cup (125 ml) marsala wine
115 g (4 ounces) shredded mozzarella cheese

- Rinse chicken pieces, pat dry and flatten to about ½ cm (¼ inch) thick with rolling pin. Dip chicken in beaten eggs and coat all sides.
- Marinate, covered, in refrigerator for several hours or overnight. Turn chicken occasionally.
- When ready to bake, preheat oven to 175°C (350° F).
- Heat oil in large frypan over medium-high heat. Dip chicken in breadcrumbs, place in frypan and brown on all sides. Drain and place in sprayed 23 x 33-cm (9 x 13-inch) baking dish.
- Spread mushrooms over chicken. Mix garlic, stock and wine in bowl and pour over chicken. Cover and bake for 30 minutes. Remove cover and bake for an additional 25 minutes.
- Sprinkle cheese over top of chicken pieces and bake for an additional 5 minutes or until cheese melts. Serves 10.

Chicken Tetrazzini

½ cup (115 g) butter
6 tablespoons (45 g) flour
800 ml (28 ounces) chicken stock
250 ml (8 ounces) whipping cream
455 g (16 ounces) linguine, cooked and drained
5–6 boneless, skinless chicken breast halves, cooked and cubed
1 cup (70 g) sliced fresh mushrooms
2 sticks celery, chopped
1 green capsicum, chopped
1 115-g (4-ounce) jar diced roasted red capsicum, drained
4–5 drops chilli sauce
½ cup (50 g) grated parmesan cheese

- Preheat oven to 175° C (350° F).
- Melt butter in saucepan over medium heat, add flour and a little salt and pepper, and stir until smooth. Gradually add stock and bring to boil. Cook and stir constantly until it thickens.
- Remove from heat and stir in cream. If sauce seems too thick, add a little milk.
- Mix 2 cups (500 ml) sauce with cooked linguine, pour into sprayed 23 x 33-cm (9 x 13-inch) baking dish and spread evenly.
- To remaining sauce, add chicken, mushrooms, celery, capsicum, roasted capsicum and chilli sauce and mix well. Pour over linguine and sprinkle with parmesan cheese.
- Cover and bake for about 45 minutes. Uncover and bake for an additional 10 minutes. Serves 10.

TIP: You can use leftover turkey instead of chicken as long as the turkey is not smoked turkey. The white meat of the turkey is better to use than the dark meat.

Blue Ribbon Chicken

3 large boneless, skinless chicken breast halves, cooked
230 g (8 ounces) mild taco sauce
Garlic powder (to taste)
230 g (8 ounces) sour cream
200 g (7 ounces) corn tortillas, torn
1½ cups (170 g) shredded cheddar cheese
Sliced jalapeno chillies
Chilli powder
2 tablespoons (30 g) butter
2 tablespoons (30 g) flour
1 cup (250 ml) milk, warmed

- Preheat oven to 175° C (350° F).
- Shred chicken breasts and mix with taco sauce. Sprinkle with a little garlic powder, salt and pepper and set aside.
- Melt butter in saucepan over medium heat, add flour and stir constantly to mix well. (Make sure there are no lumps.) Heat and stir several minutes until paste-like mixture forms.
- Pour milk into mixture, stir constantly and bring to a boil. Reduce heat to simmer, continue to stir constantly and cook about 2 minutes. Stir in a little salt and pepper and remove from heat.
- Combine sour cream and white sauce and set aside.
- Place half of tortillas in sprayed 23 x 33-cm (9 x 13-inch) baking dish. Add chicken mixture and half of sour cream mixture. Sprinkle with remaining tortillas.
- Top with remaining sour cream mixture and sprinkle with cheese. Scatter jalapeno chillies and chilli powder over top.
- Bake for 20 to 30 minutes or until it is thoroughly hot. Serves 6 to 8.

Chicken and Broccoli Casserole

8 boneless, skinless chicken breast halves, sliced
½ cup (115 g) butter
½ cup (60 g) flour
2 cups (500 ml) light cream
400 ml (14 ounces) chicken stock
230 g (8 ounces) shredded cheddar cheese
85 g (3 ounces) grated parmesan cheese
2 tablespoons (30 ml) lemon juice
1 tablespoon (15 ml) mustard
2 tablespoons (5 g) dried parsley
1 tablespoon (10 g) dried onion flakes
3 tablespoons (30 g) fresh chopped onion
¾ cup (170 g) mayonnaise
2 280-g (10-ounce) packets frozen broccoli florets, slightly cooked
200 g (7 ounces) thin spaghetti

- Preheat oven to 175° C (350° F).
- Wash chicken and dry well with paper towels. Melt butter in large saucepan or roasting pan and add flour.
- Add cream and stir constantly over medium-low heat until thick. Add chicken stock, half cheddar cheese, parmesan cheese, lemon juice, ¼ teaspoon pepper, mustard, parsley, dried and fresh onion and 2 teaspoons salt.
- Heat on low until cheeses melt. Remove from heat and add mayonnaise. Add broccoli and chicken slices to sauce.
- Cook pasta according to package directions. Drain and pour into 25 x 38-cm (10 x 15-inch) glass dish. (This will not fit in 23 x 33-cm/ 9 x 13-inch glass dish.)
- Spread sauce and chicken mixture over pasta and sprinkle remaining cheese over top. Bake for 40 minutes. Serves 6 to 8.

Chicken and Ham Lasagna

1 115-g (4-ounce) can chopped mushrooms, drained
1 large onion, chopped
¼ cup (60 g) butter
½ cup (60 g) flour
Ground nutmeg
400 ml (14 ounces) chicken stock
500 ml (1 pint) light cream
85 g (3 ounces) grated parmesan cheese
1 450-g (16-ounce) package frozen broccoli florets
9 lasagna sheets, cooked and drained
1½ cups (210 g) cooked, finely diced ham
2 cups (280 g) cooked, shredded chicken breasts
340 g (12 ounces) shredded cheddar cheese

- Preheat oven to 175° C (350° F).
- Sauté mushrooms and onion in butter in large frypan. Stir in flour, 1 teaspoon salt and ¼ teaspoon pepper and a dash of nutmeg and stir until they blend well.
- Gradually stir in stock and light cream, and cook, stirring, for about 2 minutes or until it thickens. Stir in parmesan cheese.
- Cut broccoli florets into smaller pieces and add to cream mixture.
- Spread about ½ cup (35 g) cream-broccoli mixture in sprayed 25 x 38-cm (10 x 15-inch) baking dish. Layer with 3 lasagna sheets, one-third of remaining broccoli mixture, ½ cup (70 g) ham, 1 cup (140 g) chicken and 1 cup (115 g) cheddar cheese.
- Top with 3 more lasagna sheets, one-third of broccoli mixture, 1 cup (140 g) ham, 1 cup (140 g) chicken and 1 cup (115 g) cheddar cheese. Pour in remaining noodles, chicken and cream-broccoli mixture.
- Cover and bake for 50 minutes or until it bubbles. Sprinkle with remaining cheese. Let stand for 15 minutes before cutting into squares to serve. Serves 12 to 14.

Chicken-Ham Tetrazzini

½ cup (85 g) slivered almonds, toasted
1 280-g (10-ounce) can cream of mushroom soup
1 280-g (10-ounce) can cream of chicken soup
¾ cup (175 ml) milk
2 tablespoons (30 ml) dry white wine
200 g (7 ounces) spaghetti, cooked and drained
2½ cups (350 g) cooked, diced chicken
2 cups (280 g) cooked, diced ham
½ cup (75 g) chopped green capsicum
½ cup (65 g) halved, pitted black olives
230 g (8 ounces) shredded cheddar cheese

- Preheat oven to 175° C (350° F).
- Combine almonds, soups, milk and wine in bowl. Stir in spaghetti, chicken, ham, capsicum and olives.
- Pour mixture into sprayed 23 x 33-cm (9 x 13-inch) baking dish. Sprinkle top of mixture with cheddar cheese and bake for 35 minutes or until hot and bubbly. Serves 8.

Chicken and Cheese Casserole

1 280-g (10-ounce) can cream of chicken soup
3 cups (420 g) cooked, chopped chicken or turkey
450 g (16 ounces) frozen broccoli florets, thawed
⅔ cup (150 g) mayonnaise
1 cup (115 g) shredded cheddar cheese
1½ cups (90 g) crushed cheese crackers

- Preheat oven to 175° C (350° F).
- Mix soup with ¼ cup (60 ml) water in large bowl. Add chicken, broccoli, mayonnaise and cheese and mix well.
- Pour into sprayed 3-L (3-quart) baking dish and spread cracker crumbs over top. Bake for 40 minutes. Serves 8.

Tootsie's Chicken Spectacular

This is a great recipe for leftover chicken or turkey.

2 cups (280 g) cooked, diced chicken
1 425-g (15-ounce) can green beans, drained
1 cup (165 g) cooked white rice
1 280-g (10-ounce) can cream of celery soup
½ cup (110 g) mayonnaise
½ cup (20 g) sliced water chestnuts
2 tablespoons (25 g) chopped roasted red capsicum
2 tablespoons (20 g) chopped onion

- Preheat oven to 175° C (350° F).
- Combine all ingredients with ¼ teaspoon salt and a dash of pepper in bowl and mix well.
- Place in 1½-litre (1½-quart) baking dish and bake for 25 to 30 minutes. Serves 8.

TIP: For a change, substitute cream of mushroom soup or cream of chicken soup.

Chicken-Pasta Delight

This recipe is a hearty main dish and the capsicums make it colourful as well. It's a great family supper.

2 sticks celery, chopped
½ onion, chopped
½ green capsicum, chopped
½ red capsicum, chopped
6 tablespoons (85 g) butter
3 cups (420 g) cooked, cubed chicken breasts
1 115-g (4-ounce) can sliced mushrooms, drained
1 450-g (16-ounce) jar sun-dried tomato alfredo sauce
½ cup (125 ml) unthickened cream
1½ teaspoons chicken stock powder
1 230-g (8-ounce) package fettuccini (medium egg noodles), cooked, drained

- Preheat oven to 160° C (325° F).
- Combine celery, onion, capsicum and 4 tablespoons (55 g) butter in frypan or large saucepan and sauté for about 5 minutes.
- Remove from heat and add chicken, mushrooms, alfredo sauce, cream, chicken stock and noodles and mix well. Pour into sprayed 3-L (3-quart) baking dish.

1 cup (30 g) cornflake crumbs
½ cup (60 g) shredded cheddar cheese

- Combine topping ingredients in bowl and sprinkle over casserole. Bake for 20 minutes or until casserole bubbles around edges. Serves 10.

Chicken-Risoni Florentine

4 boneless, skinless chicken breast halves
¾ cup (70 g) risoni
230 g (8 ounces) fresh mushrooms, sliced
1 280-g (10-ounce) package frozen spinach, thawed and well drained*
1 280-g (10-ounce) can mushroom soup
½ cup (110 g) mayonnaise
1 tablespoon (15 ml) lemon juice
230 g (8 ounces) shredded cheddar cheese, divided
½ cup (60 g) seasoned Italian breadcrumbs

- Preheat oven to 175° C (350° F).
- Cook chicken in boiling water for about 15 minutes and reserve broth. Cut chicken into bite-sized pieces and set aside. Pour broth through strainer and cook risoni in remaining broth.
- Sauté mushrooms in large, sprayed frypan until tender. Remove from heat and stir in chicken, risoni, spinach, soup, mayonnaise, lemon juice and ½ teaspoon pepper. Fold in half cheese and mix well.
- Spoon into sprayed 23 x 33-cm (9 x 13-inch) baking dish and sprinkle with remaining cheese and breadcrumbs. Bake for 35 minutes. Serves 8.

**TIP: Squeeze spinach between paper towels to completely remove excess moisture.*

Chicken-Sausage Extraordinaire

170 g (6 ounces) mixed long-grain and wild rice
450 g (1 pound) pork sausage
1 cup (100 g) chopped celery
2 onions, chopped
1 115-g (4-ounce) tin sliced mushrooms, drained
4 boneless, skinless, chicken breast halves, cooked, sliced
¼ cup (60 g) butter
¼ cup (30 g) flour
1 cup (250 ml) pouring cream
400 ml (14 ounces) chicken stock
1 teaspoon poultry seasoning
2 cups (120 g) crushed crackers

- Preheat oven to 175° C (350° F).
- Cook rice according to package directions and set aside.
- Brown sausage in frypan and remove with slotted spoon. Sauté celery and onions in sausage fat until onion is transparent, but not brown. Drain.
- Stir in mushrooms and chicken and set aside. Melt 3 tablespoons (45 g) of the butter in large saucepan, add flour and mix well.
- Slowly add cream, stock and poultry seasoning. Cook, stirring constantly over medium heat until mixture is fairly thick. Pour into large bowl.
- Add rice, sausage-onion mixture, chicken-mushroom mixture and ½ teaspoon each of salt and pepper. Spoon into sprayed 25 x 38-cm (10 x 15-inch) baking dish.
- Mix 1 tablespoon (15 g) melted butter and crushed crackers in bowl and sprinkle over casserole. Bake for 40 minutes or until casserole bubbles around edges. Serves 12 to 14.

TIP: This dish makes enough for about 12 to 14 people so you could easily place it in 2 smaller baking dishes and freeze one.

Alfredo Chicken

5–6 boneless, skinless chicken breast halves
Olive oil
450 g (16 ounces) frozen broccoli florets, thawed
1 red capsicum, seeded and chopped
1 455-g (16-ounce) jar alfredo sauce

- Preheat oven to 160° C (325° F).
- Brown and cook chicken breasts in large frypan with a little oil until juices run clear. Transfer to sprayed 23 x 33-cm (9 x 13-inch) baking dish.
- Microwave broccoli according to package directions and drain. Spoon broccoli and capsicum over chicken.
- Heat alfredo sauce with ¼ cup (60 ml) water in small saucepan. Pour over chicken and vegetables. Cover and bake for 15 to 20 minutes. Serves 6.

TIP: This chicken and broccoli dish can be 'dressed up' a bit by sprinkling shredded parmesan cheese on top after the casserole bakes.

Chicken-Vegetable Medley

¼ cup (60 g) plus
3 tablespoons (45 g) butter
¼ cup (30 g) flour
500 ml (1 pint) light cream
½ cup (125 ml) cooking sherry
1 280-g (10-ounce) can cream of chicken soup
1 280-g (10-ounce) package frozen broccoli, thawed
1 280-g (10-ounce) package frozen cauliflower, thawed
1 red capsicum, thinly sliced
1 cup (100 g) chopped celery
1 cup (195 g) cooked brown rice
4 cups (560 g) cooked, cubed chicken or turkey
230 g (8 ounces) shredded cheddar cheese
1 cup (60 g) soft breadcrumbs

- Preheat oven to 175° C (350° F).
- Melt ¼ cup (60 g) butter in saucepan, add flour and stir until they blend.
- Slowly stir in light cream and sherry and cook, stirring constantly, until mixture thickens. Blend in soup until mixture is smooth and set aside.
- Place broccoli, cauliflower, red capsicum and celery into sprayed 23 x 33-cm (9 x 13-inch) baking dish.
- Cover with rice, half sauce and top with chicken. Stir shredded cheese into remaining sauce and pour over chicken.
- Melt 3 tablespoons (45 g) butter and combine with breadcrumbs. Sprinkle over casserole. Bake for about 40 minutes or until casserole is thoroughly hot. Serves 12.

Chilli-Chicken Casserole

3 boneless, skinless chicken breasts, cooked, cubed
1 green capsicum, chopped
1 onion, chopped
1 115-g (4-ounce) jar chopped green chillies, drained
1 teaspoon oregano
1 teaspoon dried coriander leaves
½ teaspoon garlic powder
1 200-g (7-ounce) jar whole green chillies, drained
1½ cups (160 g) shredded cheddar cheese
1½ cups (160 g) shredded sharp cheddar cheese
3 large eggs
1 tablespoon (15 g) flour
1 cup (250 ml) unthickened cream

- Preheat oven to 175° C (350° F).
- Combine chicken with capsicum, onion, green chillies, oregano, coriander, garlic powder and ½ teaspoon each of salt and pepper in a frypan.
- Seed whole chillies and spread into sprayed 23 x 33-cm (9 x 13-inch) baking dish. Cover with meat mixture and sprinkle with cheeses.
- Combine eggs and flour in bowl and beat with fork until fluffy. Add cream, mix well and pour over top of meat in baking dish. Bake for 30 to 35 minutes or until light brown. Serves 8.

Chinese Chicken

3½ cups (490 g) cooked, cubed chicken
2 280-g (10-ounce) cans cream of chicken soup
450 g (16 ounces) frozen stir-fry vegetables, thawed
1 230-g (8-ounce) can sliced water chestnuts, drained
¾ cup (105 g) cashew nuts
1 cup (150 g) chopped green capsicum
1 bunch spring onions with tops, sliced
½ cup (50 g) chopped celery
⅓ teaspoon chilli sauce
¼ teaspoon curry powder
145 g (5 ounces) chow mein noodles

- Preheat oven to 175° C (350° F).
- Combine chicken, soup, vegetables, water chestnuts, cashew nuts, capsicum, spring onions, celery, chilli sauce and curry powder in large bowl. Stir to mix well.
- Spoon mixture into sprayed 23 x 33-cm (9 x 13-inch) glass baking dish and sprinkle chow mein noodles over casserole.
- Bake for 30 to 35 minutes or until bubbly at edges. Set aside for about 5 minutes before serving. Serves 8.

Chinese Garden

It is stretching a point to call this Chinese, but the combination of ingredients makes a great-tasting casserole.

1 170-g (6-ounce) package Oriental fried rice
2 tablespoons (30 g) butter
1 onion, chopped
2 cups (200 g) chopped celery
½ cup (70 g) slivered almonds
1 425-g (15-ounce) can Chinese vegetables, drained
1 230-g (8-ounce) can sliced bamboo shoots
3½ cups (500 g) cooked, chopped chicken
1 280-g (10-ounce) can cream of chicken soup
1 cup (225 g) mayonnaise
2 tablespoons (30 ml) soy sauce
½ teaspoon garlic powder
1 cup (55 g) chow mein noodles

- Preheat oven to 175° C (350° F).
- Cook rice according to package directions and set aside.
- Heat butter in large frypan and saute onion and celery. Add almonds, Chinese vegetables, bamboo shoots and chicken and mix well.
- Heat chicken soup, mayonnaise, soy sauce, garlic powder and a little pepper in saucepan just enough to mix well.
- Combine rice, vegetable-chicken mixture and soup mixture in large bowl and mix well. Transfer to sprayed 3-L (3-quart) baking dish.
- Sprinkle noodles over casserole. Bake for 35 minutes. Serves 8.

Comfort Chicken Plus

1 170-g (6-ounce) box chicken stuffing mix
1 bunch fresh broccoli, cut into florets
1 cup (100 g) chopped celery
1 cup (150 g) chopped red capsicum
2 tablespoons (30 g) butter
1 230-g (8-ounce) can corn, drained
2½ cups (350 g) finely chopped chicken or leftover turkey
200 ml (7 ounces) hollandaise sauce
85 g (3 ounces) onions chopped finely and fried until crispy

- Preheat oven to 160° C (325° F).
- Prepare chicken stuffing mix according to package directions.
- Place broccoli, celery, capsicum, butter and ¼ cup (60 ml) water in microwave-safe bowl. Cover with baking paper and microwave on high for 1½ minutes.
- Add broccoli-celery mixture, corn and chicken to stuffing and mix well. Spoon into sprayed 23 x 33-cm (9 x 13-inch) baking dish.
- Add 100 ml (3½ ounces) water to hollandaise sauce, pour over casserole and sprinkle top with onions. Bake for 25 minutes. Serves 8.

Creamed Chicken and Rice

4 cups (380 g) cooked instant rice
6 tablespoons (85 g) butter
¼ cup (30 g) flour
2 cups (500 ml) milk
2 teaspoons chicken stock powder
1 teaspoon dried parsley flakes
½ teaspoon celery salt
4 cups (560 g) cooked, cubed chicken
450 g (16 ounces) shredded processed cheese
230 g (8 ounces) sour cream
1½ cups (90 g) round, buttery crackers, crumbled

- Preheat oven to 160° C (325° F).
- Spread cooked rice into sprayed 23 x 33-cm (9 x 13-inch) baking dish and set aside.
- Melt 4 tablespoons (55 g) butter in large saucepan, stir in flour and mix until smooth. Gradually add milk, stock powder, seasonings and ½ teaspoon salt.
- Cook, stirring constantly, on medium heat for about 2 minutes or until sauce thickens.
- Reduce heat and add chicken, cheese and sour cream and stir until cheese melts.
- Spoon over rice in baking dish. Melt remaining 2 tablespoons (30 g) butter and toss with cracker crumbs. Sprinkle over casserole.
- Bake for 35 minutes or until hot. Serves 8.

Chicken Soufflé

16 slices white bread, crusts removed
Butter, softened
5 boneless, skinless chicken breast halves, cooked, thinly sliced diagonally
½ cup (110 g) mayonnaise
1 cup (110 g) shredded cheddar cheese, divided
5 large eggs
2 cups (500 ml) milk
1 280-g (10-ounce) can cream of mushroom soup

- Line 8 slices of bread, buttered on 1 side, in sprayed 23 x 33-cm (9 x 13-inch) baking dish. Cover with sliced chicken.
- Spread chicken slices with mayonnaise and sprinkle with ½ cup (60 g) cheese. Top with remaining 8 slices bread.
- Beat eggs, milk and ½ teaspoon each of salt and pepper in bowl and pour over entire casserole. Refrigerate all day or overnight.
- When ready to bake, preheat oven to 175° C (350° F). Spread mushroom soup with back of large spoon over top of casserole. Cover and bake for 45 minutes.
- Uncover, sprinkle with remaining cheddar cheese, return to oven and bake for an additional 15 minutes. Serves 8.

TIP: To save time, you could use deli-sliced chicken instead of cooking the chicken breasts.

Spicy Chicken-Enchilada Casserole

1 onion, chopped
2 tablespoons (30 ml) olive oil
1 425-g (15-ounce) can tomatoes with juice
1 230-g (8-ounce) jar tomato simmer sauce
1 115-g (4-ounce) can chopped green chillies
1 30-g (1-ounce) packet enchilada or taco seasoning mix
1 clove garlic, minced
3–4 cups (420–560 g) cooked, shredded chicken
12 corn tortillas
1 115-g (4-ounce) jar sliced black olives
450 g (16 ounces) shredded cheddar cheese

- Preheat oven to 175° C (350° F).
- Sauté onion with oil in large roasting pan until translucent, but not brown. Add tomatoes, simmer sauce, green chillies, enchilada seasoning mix, garlic, ½ teaspoon salt and chicken. Bring to a boil, turn heat down and simmer for 15 minutes.
- Place 4 tortillas in sprayed 23 x 33-cm (9 x 13-inch) baking pan and spread evenly with one-third of the chicken mixture over the top. Add one-third of the olives and 1 cup (110 g) cheese and spread evenly. Repeat layers twice, but reserve final layer of cheese.
- Cover and bake for 35 minutes. Uncover and sprinkle remaining cheese over top. Return to oven for 5 minutes. Serves 8 to 10.

Easy Chicken and Dumplings

3 cups (420 g) cooked, chopped chicken
2 280-g (10-ounce) cans cream of chicken soup
3 teaspoons chicken stock powder
150 g (5 ounces) scone mix

- Combine chopped chicken, both cans of soup, chicken stock powder and 4½ cups (1.1 L) water in large soup pot or large, heavy pan. Boil mixture and stir to mix well.
- Prepare the scone mix according to the directions on the packet. Drop teaspoonfuls of the dough into the boiling chicken mixture and stir gently.
- When all scones are in pot, reduce heat to low, simmer and stir occasionally for about 20 minutes. Serves 8.

TIP: Deli turkey will also work in this recipe. It's a great time-saver!

Family Chicken Bake

This is a great, basic 'meat-and-potato' dish that all families love.

¼ cup (60 g) butter
1 red capsicum, chopped
1 onion, chopped
2 sticks celery, chopped
230 g (8 ounces) sour cream
1½ cups (375 ml) light cream
1 200-g (7-ounce) jar chopped green chillies, drained
1 teaspoon chicken stock powder
½ teaspoon celery salt
3–4 cups (420–560 g) cooked, cubed chicken
450 g (16 ounces) shredded cheddar cheese
900 g (2 pounds) frozen hash browns, thawed and shredded

- Preheat oven to 175° C (350° F).
- Melt butter in saucepan and sauté capsicum, onion and celery. Combine sour cream, cream, green chillies, stock, celery salt and ½ teaspoon each of salt and pepper in large bowl.
- Stir in capsicum mixture, chicken and half of cheese. Fold in hash browns. Spoon into sprayed 23 x 33-cm (9 x 13-inch) baking dish.
- Bake for 45 minutes or until casserole is bubbly. Remove from oven and sprinkle remaining cheese over top of casserole. Return to oven for about 5 minutes. Serves 12 to 14.

TIP: For a change of pace, heat some hot, thick, chunky salsa to spoon over the top of each serving.

Family Night Spaghetti

This recipe has a little different twist on the ever-popular chicken spaghetti. This is a wonderful casserole to serve to family or for guests. It has great flavour with chicken, pasta and colourful vegetables all in one dish. It's a real winner!

1 bunch spring onions with tops, chopped
1 cup (100 g) chopped celery
1 red capsicum, chopped
1 yellow or orange capsicum, chopped
¼ cup (60 g) butter
1 tablespoon (2 g) dried coriander leaves
1 teaspoon Italian seasoning
230 g (8 ounces) thin spaghetti, cooked and drained
4 cups (560 g) cooked, chopped chicken or turkey
230 g (8 ounces) sour cream
1 455-g (16-ounce) jar creamy alfredo sauce
280 g (10 ounces) frozen green peas, thawed
230 g (8 ounces) shredded mozzarella cheese

- Preheat oven to 175° C (350° F).
- Sauté onions, celery and capsicums in butter in large frypan. Combine onion-capsicum mixture, coriander, Italian seasoning, spaghetti, chicken, sour cream and alfredo sauce in large bowl and mix well.
- Sprinkle a little salt and pepper into the mixture. Fold in peas and half mozzarella cheese. Spoon into sprayed 25 x 38-cm (10 x 15-inch) deep baking dish. Cover and bake for 45 minutes. Uncover and sprinkle remaining cheese over casserole. Return to oven for about 5 minutes. Serves 8 to 10.

TIP: If you want another twist, use chopped, cooked ham instead of chicken.

Garden Chicken

This colourful, delicious casserole is not only flavour packed, but it is also a sight to behold! You can't beat this bountiful dish for family or guests.

4 boneless, skinless chicken breasts halves, cut into strips
1 teaspoon minced garlic
6 tablespoons (90 g) butter
1 small yellow squash, thinly sliced
1 small zucchini, thinly sliced
1 red capsicum, thinly sliced
4 tablespoons (30 g) flour
2 teaspoons pesto
400 ml (14 ounces) chicken stock
1 cup (250 ml) light cream
230 g (8 ounces) angel hair pasta, cooked al dente and drained
⅓ cup (35 g) shredded parmesan cheese

- Preheat oven to 175° C (350° F).
- Sauté chicken and garlic in 3 tablespoons (45 g) butter in large frypan over medium heat for about 15 minutes. Remove ingredients and set aside.
- With butter that is left in frypan, sauté squash, zucchini and capsicum and cook just until tender but crisp.
- Melt 3 tablespoons (45 g) butter in small saucepan and add flour, pesto and ½ teaspoon (2 ml) each of salt and pepper. Stir to form smooth paste.
- Gradually add stock, stirring constantly over medium-high heat, until thick. Stir in cream and heat thoroughly.
- Combine chicken, vegetables, broth-cream mixture and drained pasta in large bowl. Transfer to sprayed 23 x 33-cm (9 x 13-inch) baking dish.
- Cover and bake for 30 minutes.
- Uncover and sprinkle parmesan cheese over top of casserole, then return to oven for an additional 5 minutes. Serves 8.

Great Crazy Lasagna

Chicken never got mixed up with any better ingredients!

1 tablespoon (15 g) butter
½ onion, chopped
1 cup (70 g) sliced fresh mushrooms
1 280-g (10-ounce) can cream of chicken soup
1 455-g (16-ounce) jar alfredo sauce
1 115-g (4-ounce) jar roasted red capsicums, drained
⅓ cup (75 ml) dry white wine
280 g (10 ounces) frozen chopped spinach, thawed
425 g (15 ounces) ricotta cheese
⅓ cup (35 g) grated parmesan cheese
1 egg, beaten
9 lasagna sheets, cooked
3–4 cups (420–560 g) cooked, shredded chicken
450 g (16 ounces) shredded cheddar cheese

- Preheat oven to 175° C (350° F).
- Melt butter and sauté onion and mushrooms in large frypan. Stir in soup, alfredo sauce, capsicum and wine. Reserve one-third sauce for top of lasagna.
- Squeeze spinach between paper towels to completely remove excess moisture. Combine spinach, ricotta, parmesan and egg in bowl and mix well.
- Place 3 lasagna sheets in sprayed 25 x 38-cm (10 x 15-inch) baking dish.
- Layer each with half of remaining sauce, spinach-ricotta mixture and chicken. (The spinach-ricotta mixture will be fairly dry.)
- Sprinkle with 1½ cups (175 g) cheddar cheese. Repeat layering. Top with last 3 lasagna sheets and reserved sauce.
- Cover and bake for 45 minutes. Uncover and sprinkle remaining cheese on top. Return to oven and bake for an additional 5 minutes. Let lasagna stand for 10 minutes. Serves 12 to 14.

Green Chilli-Chicken Enchilada Casserole

This classic casserole is good for all occasions. If you don't want to cook a whole chicken, use 6 to 8 boneless, skinless chicken breast halves. It will save you some time.

1 whole chicken
1 large onion, chopped
3 sticks celery, chopped
1 tablespoon (15 g) butter
1 200-g (7-ounce) can chopped green chillies
1 cup (250 ml) milk
1 280-g (10-ounce) can cream of chicken soup
1 280-g (10-ounce) can cream of mushroom soup
10 corn tortillas, cut into strips
340 g (12 ounces) shredded cheddar cheese

- Preheat oven to 175° C (350° F).
- Bake chicken in covered baking dish with 1½ cups (375 ml) water, onion, celery, butter, and a little salt and pepper for 1 hour or until juices run clear.
- Remove from oven, remove chicken to platter to cool and reserve 1 cup (250 ml) chicken stock. When chicken cools, remove meat from bone.
- Combine green chillies, milk, reserved chicken stock, chicken soup and mushroom soup in saucepan and heat just enough to mix.
- Place half of tortillas in sprayed 23 x 33-cm (9 x 13-inch) baking dish, cover with half chicken and half soup mixture and repeat layers.
- Cover and bake for about 30 minutes. Uncover and sprinkle cheese on top of casserole and bake for an additional 5 minutes. Serves 10.

Sizzling Chicken Pepe

2 280-g (10-ounce) cans cream of chicken soup
1 cup (250 ml) milk
1 30-g (1-ounce) packet taco seasoning
1 115-g (4-ounce) jar chopped green chillies
280 g (10 ounces) corn chips
5–6 boneless, skinless chicken breasts, cooked, cubed
450 g (16 ounces) shredded cheddar cheese

- Preheat oven to 160° C (325° F).
- Combine soup, milk, taco seasoning and green chillies in bowl.
- Make 2 layers of following ingredients in 23 x 33-cm (9 x 13-inch) glass baking dish: chips, chicken, soup mixture and cheese. Bake for 1 hour. Serves 6.

So Simple Chicken and Rice

4–6 boneless, skinless chicken breast halves
Seasoning salt
1 cup (95 g) rice
1 30-g (1-ounce) packet onion soup mix

- Preheat oven to 175°C (350° F).
- Sprinkle chicken with seasoning salt and a little pepper. Place rice in sprayed 23 x 33-cm (9 x 13-inch) baking dish and place chicken on top.
- Mix 1½ cups (375 ml) water with onion soup mix and pour over chicken. Cover and bake for 1 hour 30 minutes. Serves 4 to 6.

Chicken-Cashew Bake

⅓ cup (55 g) minced onion
1 cup (100 g) minced celery
1 tablespoon (15 g) butter, melted
1 280-g (10-ounce) can cream of mushroom soup
½ cup (125 ml) chicken stock
1 tablespoon (15 ml) soy sauce
3 drops Tabasco sauce
2 cups (280 g) cooked, diced chicken
1 cup (55 g) chow mein noodles
½ cup (70 g) chopped cashew nuts

- Preheat oven to 175° C (350° F).
- Sauté onion and celery in butter in saucepan. Add soup and chicken stock. Stir in soy sauce, Tabasco sauce and chicken and simmer for about 5 minutes.
- Pour into 1-L (1-quart) baking dish. Sprinkle noodles and nuts on top.
- Bake for 20 minutes or until thoroughly hot. Serves 4 to 6.

Jazzy Turkey and Dressing

1 230-g (8-ounce) package chicken stuffing mix
3 cups (420 g) cooked, diced turkey
1 425-g (15-ounce) can corn, drained
1 115-g (4-ounce) jar chopped green chillies, drained
½ cup (75 g) chopped red capsicum
2 tablespoons (4 g) dried parsley flakes
1 280-g (10-ounce) can cream of chicken soup
230 g (8 ounces) sour cream
2 tablespoons (30 g) butter, melted
2 teaspoons ground cumin
1 cup (115 g) shredded mozzarella cheese

- Preheat oven to 175° C (350° F).
- Combine all ingredients, except cheese, in large mixing bowl with ½ cup (125 ml) water and ½ teaspoon salt and mix well.
- Pour into sprayed 23 x 33-cm (9 x 13-inch) baking dish. Cover and bake for 35 minutes.
- Uncover, sprinkle with cheese and bake for 5 minutes.
  Serves 10.

Jalapeno Chicken Bark

This one barks a little to get your attention, but it really is good.

5–6 boneless, skinless chicken breast halves
¼ cup (60 ml) oil
¼ cup (60 ml) white wine
450 g (1 pint) sour cream
1 tablespoon (10 g) flour
1 clove garlic, minced
½ teaspoon ground cumin
1 200-g (7-ounce) jar jalapeno chillies
340 g (12 ounces) shredded cheddar cheese
1 onion, sliced in rounds

- Preheat oven to 160° C (325° F).
- Brown chicken on both sides in oil in a frypan. Place in a 23 x 33-cm (9 x 13-inch) baking dish.
- Combine wine, sour cream, flour, garlic, ½ teaspoon salt, ¼ teaspoon pepper, cumin and chillies in blender.
- Blend until smooth to make sauce. Pour sauce over chicken breasts, sprinkle with cheese and top with onion rings. Cover and bake for 1 hour. Serves 6.

TIP: If you like it extra hot, leave the seeds in the jalapenos. If you take the seeds out, rubber gloves will protect your hands from the juices.

Jalapeno Chicken

Even if you're not a spinach fan, you will find this to your liking!

2 cups (320 g) chopped onion
2 tablespoons (30 g) butter
1 280-g (10-ounce) package frozen spinach, cooked, drained
6 jalapeno chillies or 1 200-g (7-ounce) jar green chillies, drained
230 g (8 ounces) sour cream
2 280-g (10-ounce) cans cream of chicken soup
4 spring onions with tops, chopped
340 g (12 ounces) corn chips, slightly crushed
4 cups (560 g) cooked, diced turkey or chicken
230 g (8 ounces) shredded cheddar cheese

- Preheat oven to 175° C (350° F).
- Sauté onion in butter in saucepan and blend in spinach, green chillies, sour cream, soups, onions and ½ teaspoon salt.
- Layer chips, chicken, spinach mixture and cheese in large 25 x 38-cm (10 x 15-inch) baking dish or two 23 x 23-cm (9 x 9-inch) dishes. Repeat process with cheese on top. Bake for 35 minutes. Serves 12.

Jolly Ol' Chicken

With this casserole, you have the chicken and cranberry sauce all in one dish.

170 g (6 ounces) long-grain and wild rice mix, cooked
450 g (16 ounces) whole-berry cranberry sauce
⅓ cup (85 ml) orange juice
3 tablespoons (45 g) butter, melted
½ teaspoon curry powder
6 boneless, skinless chicken breast halves, cooked
⅔ cup (110 g) slivered almonds

- Preheat oven to 160° C (325° F).
- Pour rice into sprayed 23 x 33-cm (9 x 13-inch) baking dish.
- Combine cranberry sauce, orange juice, butter and curry powder in saucepan and heat just enough to mix ingredients well.
- Place chicken over rice and pour cranberry-orange juice mixture over chicken.
- Cover and bake for about 10 to 15 minutes.
- Uncover, sprinkle almonds over casserole and return to oven for about 10 to 15 minutes, just until chicken is light brown. Serves 8.

King Ranch Chicken

8 20-cm (8-inch) corn tortillas
Chicken stock
1 onion, chopped
1 green capsicum, chopped
2 tablespoons (30 g) butter
1 280-g (10-ounce) can cream of chicken soup
1 280-g (10-ounce) can cream of mushroom soup
1 tablespoon (15 g) chilli powder
1–1.5 kg (2–3 pounds) chicken cooked, diced
340 g (12 ounces) shredded cheese
1 280-g (10-ounce) can chopped tomatoes
60 g (2 ounces) green chillies, chopped

- Preheat oven to 175° C (350° F).
- Dip half of tortillas in hot chicken stock just long enough to soften and place in sprayed 25 x 38-cm (10 x 15-inch) baking dish.
- Sauté onion and capsicum with butter in frypan. Stir in soups, chilli powder and diced chicken.
- Pour layer of half soup-chicken mixture over tortillas and half cheese. Repeat layers and spread tomatoes and green chillies over casserole.
- Bake for 40 to 45 minutes or until hot and bubbly. Serves 12.

Don't Be Chicken Casserole

2 cups (110 g) crushed corn chips
4 boneless, skinless chicken breast halves, cooked
1 425-g (15-ounce) can chickpeas, drained
1 425-g (15-ounce) can borlotti beans, drained
1 425-g (15-ounce) can corn, drained
1 455-g (16-ounce) jar hot salsa
1 red onion, chopped
2 teaspoons ground cumin
1 teaspoon dried coriander leaves
1 green capsicum, diced
2 teaspoons minced garlic
230 g (8 ounces) shredded mozzarella cheese, divided
230 g (8 ounces) shredded sharp cheddar cheese
Tomato slices (optional)
Sour cream (optional)
Spring onions (optional)

- Preheat oven to 175° C (350° F).
- Scatter crushed corn chips evenly in sprayed 23 x 33-cm (9 x 13-inch) baking dish.
- Cut chicken breasts in thin slices. Combine chicken, chickpeas, beans, corn, salsa, onion, cumin, coriander, capsicum, garlic and 1 teaspoon salt in large bowl and mix well.
- Spoon half of mixture evenly over chips.
- Combine cheeses in bowl and sprinkle half over mixture. Cover with remaining half of chicken-bean mixture and remaining cheese.
- Bake for 35 minutes. Let stand for 10 minutes before serving. Garnish with tomato slices, sour cream and chopped spring onions, if you like.

Serves 8 to 10.

Mexican Turkey Fiesta

If you use leftover turkey for this recipe, all you have to do to have a delicious casserole is to cut up your turkey, an onion and a capsicum. The rest is opening cans and a bag of chips!

4 cups (560 g) deli chopped turkey
1 onion, chopped
340 g (12 ounces) shredded cheddar cheese
1 green capsicum, chopped
1 teaspoon chilli powder
½ teaspoon ground cumin
2 280-g (10-ounce) cans cream of chicken soup
1 280-g (10-ounce) can diced tomatoes
60 g (2 ounces) green chillies, sliced
370 g (13 ounces) corn chips

- Preheat oven to 160° C (325° F).
- Combine all ingredients in large pan except corn chips. Add ½ teaspoon each of salt and pepper and mix well.
- Pour two-thirds corn chips into sprayed 23 x 23-cm (9 x 13-inch) baking dish and crush slightly with hands.
- Pour all turkey-cheese mixture over crushed chips and spread out. Crush remaining chips and spread over casserole. Bake for 40 minutes. Serves 10.

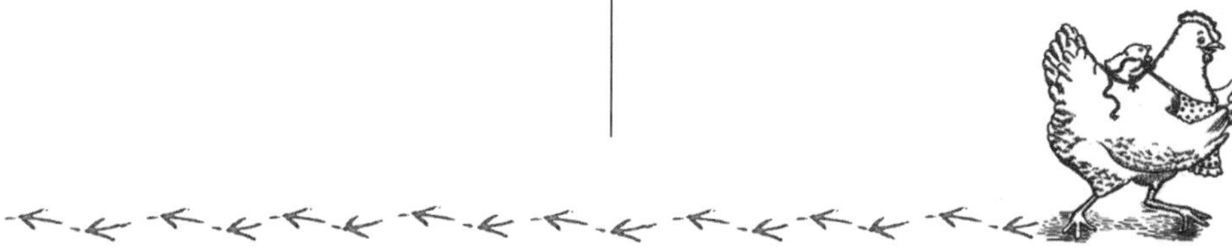

Not JUST Chicken

This is a great recipe for leftover ham or turkey. It is really a 'quick fix' for the family.

3 cups (420 g) cooked, cubed chicken or turkey
3 cups (420 g) fully cooked, cubed ham
230 g (8 ounces) shredded cheddar cheese
1 425-g (15-ounce) can baby peas, drained
1 onion, chopped
3 sticks celery, chopped
¼ cup (60 g) butter
⅓ cup (40 g) plus 1 tablespoon (10 g) flour
500 ml (1 pint) light cream
½ cup (125 ml) milk
1 teaspoon dill
Instant brown rice, cooked

- Preheat oven to 175° C (350° F).
- Combine chicken, ham, cheese and peas in large bowl.
- Sauté onion and celery in butter in very large saucepan until tender. Add flour and stir to make a paste.
- Gradually add cream, milk, dill and 1 teaspoon salt. Heat, stirring constantly, until mixture thickens.
- Add thickened cream mixture to chicken-ham mixture and mix well.
- Spoon into sprayed 4-L (4-quart) baking dish that you can take to the table.
- Cover and bake for 20 minutes. Spoon chicken and ham casserole over hot brown rice. Serves 12.

Old-Fashioned Chicken Spaghetti

This is a great recipe for leftover chicken or turkey.

230–280 g (8–10 ounces) spaghetti
1 green capsicum, chopped
1 onion, chopped
1 cup (100 g) chopped celery
½ cup (115 g) butter
1 280-g (10-ounce) can tomato soup
1 280-g (10-ounce) can diced tomatoes
60 g (2 ounces) green chillies, sliced
1 115-g (4-ounce) can chopped mushrooms
½ teaspoon garlic powder
3 teaspoons chicken stock powder
4–5 cups (560–700 g) cooked, chopped chicken or turkey
230 g (8 ounces) cubed mozzarella cheese
230 g (8 ounces) shredded cheddar cheese

- Preheat oven to 160° C (325° F).
- Cook pasta according to package directions and drain.
- Sauté capsicum, onion and celery in butter in medium saucepan.
- Add soup, tomatoes, green chillies, mushrooms, garlic powder, stock powder and ½ cup (125 ml) water and mix well.
- Mix pasta, soup, tomato mixture, chicken and cheeses in large mixing bowl. Place in sprayed 2-L (2 quart) baking dishes.
- Cover and bake one dish for 40 to 50 minutes. Freeze the other dish for later. To cook frozen dish, thaw first. Serves 12.

Orange-Spiced Chicken

⅔ cup (80 g) flour
½ teaspoon dried basil
¼ teaspoon French tarragon
2–3 tablespoons (30–45 ml) olive oil
6 boneless, skinless, chicken breast halves
200 ml (6½ ounces) orange juice
½ cup (125 ml) white wine vinegar
⅔ cup (150 g) packed brown sugar
170 g (6 ounces) long-grain and wild rice mix, cooked

- Preheat oven to 175° C (350° F).
- Mix flour, 1 teaspoon salt, ½ teaspoon pepper and spices in resealable plastic bag. Pour oil into large frypan and heat. Coat chicken in flour mixture and brown both sides of chicken.
- Mix orange juice, ¼ cup (60 ml) water, vinegar and brown sugar in small bowl. When chicken breasts brown, place in sprayed 23 x 33-cm (9 x 13-inch) baking dish, cover with orange juice mixture and bake for 1 hour. Serve chicken and orange sauce over rice. Serves 6.

Poppy Seed Chicken

8 boneless, skinless chicken breast halves
1 280-g (10-ounce) can cream of chicken soup
230 g (8 ounces) sour cream
½ cup (125 ml) dry white wine or cooking wine
1½ cups (90 g) round buttery crackers, crumbled
1 cup (85 g) chopped almonds, toasted
½ cup (115 g) butter, melted
2–3 tablespoons (20–25 g) poppy seeds
Rice or noodles, cooked

- Preheat oven to 175° C (350° F).
- Place chicken in sprayed 23 x 33-cm (9 x 13-inch) baking pan and set aside.
- Combine soup, sour cream and wine in saucepan and heat just until it mixes. Pour soup mixture over chicken.
- Combine cracker crumbs, almonds and butter in bowl and sprinkle over casserole. Sprinkle with poppy seeds and bake for 45 minutes. Serve over rice or noodles. Serves 8.

Pollo Delicioso

4 fresh jalapeno chillies, seeded and diced
1 onion, chopped
1 green capsicum, chopped
1 clove garlic, minced
2 tablespoons (30 ml) oil
1 teaspoon ground cumin
½ teaspoon chilli powder
1 280-g (10-ounce) can cream of chicken soup
1 280-g (10-ounce) package frozen spinach, thawed
500 ml (1 pint) sour cream
4 large boneless, skinless chicken breast halves, cooked, cubed
370 g (13 ounces) corn chips
450 g (16 ounces) shredded cheddar cheese

- Preheat oven to 160° C (325° F).
- Sauté chillies, onion, capsicum and garlic in oil in large frypan. Stir in cumin, chilli powder and chicken soup.
- Squeeze spinach between paper towels to completely remove excess moisture. Fold spinach, ½ teaspoon salt, sour cream and chicken into mixture. Heat, stirring constantly, but do not boil.
- Layer one-third corn chips, one-third cheese and one-half chicken mixture in sprayed 23 x 33-cm (9 x 13-inch) baking dish. Repeat layering and top with last layer of corn chips and cheese.
- Bake for 40 minutes or until casserole is hot and bubbly. Serves 10.

TIP: Wear rubber gloves when removing seeds from jalapeno chillies. If you like it hot, leave the seeds in.

Pow Wow Chicken

3 onions, chopped
3 green capsicums, chopped
1 teaspoon garlic powder
Olive oil
2 280-g (10-ounce) cans chopped tomatoes
60 g (2 ounces) green chillies, sliced
450 g (16 ounces) cubed mozzarella cheese
340 g (12 ounces) shredded cheddar cheese
6 cups (840 g) cooked, chopped chicken
500 ml (1 pint) sour cream
1 115-g (4-ounce) jar roasted red capsicum
Rice, cooked
Corn chips, crushed

- Cook onion, capsicums and garlic in a little oil in frypan. Add tomatoes and green chillies and bring to boil. Reduce heat and simmer for about 15 to 20 minutes or until slightly thick.
- Add cheeses; stir constantly and heat slowly until cheeses melt. Add chicken, sour cream and roasted red capsicum. Heat until hot, but do not boil.
- To serve, place rice on individual plate and top with a few crushed chips. Spoon chicken-cheese mixture over rice and chips. Serve immediately. Serves 12.

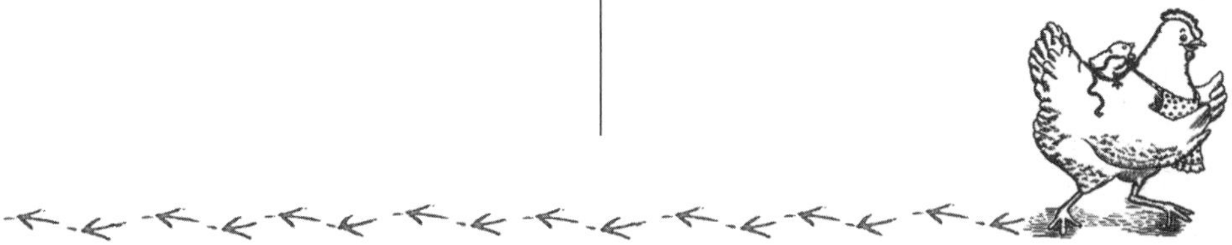

Red Rock Taco Chicken

This is a great recipe for leftover chicken.

3 cups (420 g) cooked, chopped chicken
1 30-g (1-ounce) packet taco seasoning
1 cup (95 g) white rice
2 cups (200 g) chopped celery
1 red capsicum, seeded, chopped
2 425-g (15-ounce) cans stewed tomatoes
170 g (6 ounces) onions, finely sliced and fried until crispy

- Preheat oven to 160° C (325° F).
- Combine cooked chicken, taco seasoning, rice, ½ cup (125 ml) water, celery, capsicum and tomatoes in large bowl. Transfer to sprayed 23 x 33-cm (9 x 13-inch) baking dish.
- Cover and bake for 25 minutes, then remove cover and sprinkle onion rings over casserole. Return to oven for 15 minutes. Serves 8.

Chicky Chicken with Red Capsicum

400 ml (14 ounces) chicken stock
1 230-g (8-ounce) can corn, drained
2 cups (280 g) cooked, cubed chicken breasts
1 cup (135 g) roasted red capsicum
¼ cup (30 g) pine nuts, toasted

- Preheat oven to 160° C (325° F).
- Combine chicken stock, corn, chicken and roasted capsicums in saucepan over medium-high heat. Cover and simmer for about 10 minutes.
- Spoon into sprayed 18 x 28-cm (7 x 11-inch) baking dish, top with pine nuts and bake for 15 minutes. Serves 6.

Seasoned Chicken over Tex-Mex Corn

2 teaspoons garlic powder
1 teaspoon ground cumin
⅔ cup (80 g) flour
4 boneless, skinless chicken breast halves
Olive oil
280 ml (10 ounces) chicken stock
50 g (1½ ounces) red capsicum, finely chopped
1½ cups (395 g) hot salsa
1 310-g (11-ounce) can corn
1 cup (95 g) instant rice

- Combine garlic powder, cumin, flour and ample salt in shallow bowl. Dip chicken in flour mixture and coat each side of chicken.
- Place a little oil in heavy frypan over medium-high heat. Cut each chicken breast in half lengthwise. Brown each piece on both sides, reduce heat and add 2 tablespoons (30 ml) water to pan.
- Cover and simmer for 15 minutes. Transfer chicken to foil-lined baking pan and place in oven at 120° C (250° F) to keep warm.
- Using same unwashed frypan, combine stock, salsa, corn and capsicum and cook for about 10 minutes. Stir in rice and let stand for 10 minutes or until rice is tender.
- To serve, spoon Tex-Mex Corn on platter and place chicken breasts over corn. Serves 4.

Sour Cream Chicken Enchiladas

4–5 boneless, skinless chicken breast halves
1 onion, chopped
2 tablespoons (30 g) butter
1 115-g (4-ounce) jar chopped green chillies
340 g (12 ounces) shredded cheddar cheese
2 teaspoons chilli powder
450 g (16 ounces) sour cream
10–12 tortillas
¼ cup (30 g) flour
¼ cup (60 g) butter, melted
340 g (12 ounces) shredded mozzarella cheese

- Preheat oven to 175° C (350° F).
- Cook chicken in enough water in saucepan to cover chicken, drain and reserve 1½ cups (375 ml) broth. Allow chicken to cool and chop into small pieces.
- Sauté onion in butter, add chicken, green chillies, cheddar cheese, 1 teaspoon chilli powder and 1 cup (240 g) sour cream and mix well.
- Microwave tortillas on high for about 1 minute or until softened. Spoon a little chicken-cheese mixture onto each tortilla and roll to enclose filling.
- Place seam-side down in sprayed 25 x 38-cm (10 x 15-inch) baking pan.
- Combine flour and melted butter in saucepan, mix well and add 1½ cups (375 ml) reserved broth Cook, stirring constantly, until thick and bubbly.
- Fold in one-half mozzarella cheese, remaining sour cream and remaining chilli powder. Spoon over enchiladas.
- Bake for 30 minutes. Remove from oven and sprinkle with remaining cheese. Serves 12.

Chicken-Broccoli Deluxe

½ cup (115 g) butter
½ cup (60 g) flour
400 ml (14 ounces) chicken stock
500 ml (1 pint) light cream
450 g (16 ounces) shredded cheddar cheese
145 g (5 ounces) grated parmesan cheese
2 tablespoons (30 ml) lemon juice
2 tablespoons (5 g) dried parsley
¾ cup (170 g) mayonnaise
560 g (20 ounces) frozen broccoli florets, cooked
5 boneless, skinless chicken breast halves, cooked and sliced
340 g (12 ounces) vermicelli

- Preheat oven to 160° C (325° F).
- Melt butter in very large saucepan or roasting pan. Add flour and mix. Gradually add chicken stock and light cream, stirring constantly over medium-low heat until it thickens.
- Add half cheddar cheese, parmesan cheese, lemon juice, dried parsley, 1 teaspoon salt and ½ teaspoon pepper. Heat on low until cheeses melt. Remove from heat and add mayonnaise.
- Gently add broccoli and chicken slices to sauce.
- Cook pasta according to package directions, drain and pour into sprayed 25 x 38-cm (10 x 15-inch) baking dish. Spoon sauce and chicken mixture over pasta.
- Cover and bake for 40 minutes. Uncover and spread remaining cheese over top. Return to oven for an additional 5 minutes. Serves 12.

Eggcellent Chicken Pie

340 g (12 ounces) shredded cheddar cheese
1 280-g (10-ounce) package frozen, chopped broccoli florets, thawed
2 cups (280 g) cooked, finely diced chicken breasts
½ cup (80 g) finely chopped onion
½ cup (75 g) finely chopped red capsicum
1⅓ cups (335 ml) light cream
3 eggs
¾ cup (90 g) scone mix

- Preheat oven to 190° C (375° F).
- Combine 2 cups (230 g) cheddar cheese, broccoli, chicken, onion and capsicum in bowl. Spread into sprayed 25-cm (10-inch) deep-dish pie pan.
- Beat light cream, eggs, scone mix and a little salt and pepper in bowl. Slowly pour cream-egg mixture over broccoli-chicken mixture, but do not stir.
- Cover and bake for 35 minutes. Uncover and sprinkle remaining cheese over top. Return to oven for about 5 minutes or just until cheese melts. Serves 8.

Q: What happens when you drop a hand gren-egg?

A: It egg-plodes.

Sour Cream Chicken Casserole

5 boneless, skinless chicken breast halves, cooked, cubed
450 g (1 pint) sour cream
200 g (7 ounces) spaghetti
2 280-g (10-ounce) cans cream of chicken soup
1 115-g (4-ounce) can mushrooms, drained
½ cup (115 g) butter, melted
145 g (5 ounces) grated parmesan cheese

- Preheat oven to 160° C (325° F).
- Combine all ingredients with ⅛ teaspoon pepper in bowl.
- Pour into sprayed 23 x 33-cm (9 x 13-inch) baking dish. Sprinkle extra cheese on top. Cover and bake for 50 minutes. Serves 8.

Quickie Island Chicken

This is great when you don't have time to cook.

6 boneless, skinless chicken breast halves
250 ml (8 ounces) bottle Thousand Island salad dressing
340 g (12 ounces) apricot jam
1 30-g (1-ounce) packet onion soup mix

- Preheat oven to 175° C (350° F).
- Place chicken breasts in sprayed 23 x 33-cm (9 x 13-inch) baking dish.
- Combine dressing, apricot jam, onion soup mix and ¼ cup (60 ml) water in saucepan and bring to slow boil. Remove from heat and pour over chicken.
- Cover and bake for 1 hour. Uncover, baste with sauce and bake for an additional 30 minutes. Serves 6.

Spicy Orange Chicken over Noodles

450 g (1 pound) boneless, skinless chicken tenders
2 tablespoons (30 ml) olive oil
2 tablespoons (30 ml) soy sauce
1 455-g (16-ounce) package frozen stir-fry vegetables, thawed
⅔ cup (215 g) orange marmalade
1 tablespoon (15 ml) olive oil
1 tablespoon (15 ml) soy sauce
1½ teaspoons lime juice
½ teaspoon minced ginger
½ teaspoon cayenne pepper
170 g (6 ounces) chow mein noodles

- Lightly brown chicken tenders in oil in large frypan over medium-high heat. Add soy sauce and cook for an additional 3 minutes.
- Add stir-fry vegetables and cook for about 5 minutes or until vegetables are tender but crisp.
- Combine marmalade, oil, soy sauce, lime juice, minced ginger and cayenne pepper in saucepan and mix well.
- Heat and pour over stir-fry chicken and vegetables. Serve with noodles. Serves 8 to 10.

Stampede Chicken Enchiladas

This classic enchilada dish will make your herd excited. Get ready for the stampede.

3 cups (420 g) cooked, shredded chicken
1 115-g (4-ounce) jar chopped green chillies
200 g (7 ounces) chilli salsa
1 onion, minced
6 chicken stock cubes
500 ml (1 pint) pouring cream
Olive oil
10 corn tortillas
340 g (12 ounces) shredded cheddar cheese
230 g (8 ounces) sour cream

- Preheat oven to 175° C (350° F).
- Combine chicken, green chillies, chilli salsa and onion in saucepan. Place stock cubes, ½ teaspoon salt and cream in saucepan and heat until stock dissolves, but do not boil.
- Heat oil in frypan and dip each tortilla into oil for about 5 seconds to soften. Drain on paper towels. Dip each tortilla into saucepan with cream and coat each side. Fill each tortilla with chicken mixture.
- Roll and place seam-side down in sprayed 23 x 33-cm (9 x 13-inch) baking dish. Pour remaining cream over enchiladas and sprinkle with cheese. Bake for 30 to 35 minutes. When ready to serve, top with dollops of sour cream. Serves 8.

Dinner-Ready Chicken

You will have one frypan and one saucepan to wash. Within 20 minutes you will have creamy chicken plus vegetables ready to go in the oven. And the kids will love the crunchy topping.

6 boneless, skinless chicken breast halves
2 tablespoons (30 ml) olive oil
1 cup (100 g) chopped celery
2 cups (250 g) sliced zucchini
450 g (16 ounces) baby carrots
½ onion, chopped
¼ cup (60 g) plus 2 tablespoons (30 g) butter
1 280-g (10-ounce) can cream of chicken soup
1 280-g (10-ounce) can spicy tomato soup
1 cup (250 ml) milk or unthickened cream
½ teaspoon dill
1 teaspoon dried basil
1½ cups (90 g) soft breadcrumbs
½ cup (45 g) chopped walnuts

- Preheat oven to 190° C (375° F).
- Brown chicken in frypan with oil. Place chicken breasts in sprayed 23 x 33-cm (9 x 13-inch) baking dish and set aside.
- Cook celery, zucchini, carrots and onion in saucepan for about 10 minutes in ¼ cup (60 g) butter and very little water and drain.
- Combine soups, milk, dill, basil and ½ teaspoon pepper in saucepan and heat just enough to mix well.
- Spoon about ¾ cup (175 ml) soup mixture over chicken. Combine remaining soup mixture with vegetables. Spoon over chicken and soup mixture.
- Combine 2 tablespoons (30 g) melted butter, breadcrumbs and walnuts in bowl and sprinkle over casserole. Bake for 35 to 40 minutes or until topping browns lightly. Serves 10.

Sweet-and-Sour Chicken and Veggies

1 85-g (3-ounce) package chicken-flavoured ramen noodles
1 455-g (16-ounce) package frozen broccoli, cauliflower and carrots
3 boneless, skinless, chicken breast halves, cooked, cut in strips
⅔ cup (180 g) sweet-and-sour sauce
1 tablespoon (15 ml) soy sauce

- Cook noodles and vegetables in 2 cups (500 ml) water (reserve seasoning packet) in large saucepan for 3 minutes or until liquid absorbs.
- Add seasoning packet, chicken (or turkey), sweet-and-sour sauce and soy sauce. Heat on medium-low heat, stirring until all is thoroughly hot. Serves 8 to 10.

Swiss Chicken

4 boneless, skinless chicken breast halves
4 slices Swiss cheese
1 280-g (10-ounce) can cream of chicken soup
¼ cup (60 ml) dry white wine
½ cup (20 g) herb-seasoned chicken stuffing mix
¼ cup (60 g) butter, melted

- Preheat oven to 175° C (350° F).
- Arrange chicken in sprayed 23 x 33-cm (9 x 13-inch) pan. Top with cheese. Combine soup and wine in bowl and stir well.
- Spoon evenly over chicken and sprinkle with stuffing mix. Drizzle butter over crumbs. Bake for 45 to 55 minutes. Serves 4.

Sweet Capsicum Chicken

6–8 boneless, skinless chicken breast halves
2 tablespoons (30 ml) olive oil
⅓ cup (45 g) cornflour
⅔ cup (135 g) sugar
½ cup (110 g) packed brown sugar
1 teaspoon chicken stock powder
1 425-g (15-ounce) can pineapple chunks with natural juice
1½ cups (375 ml) orange juice
½ cup (125 ml) vinegar
¼ cup (70 g) ketchup
2 tablespoons (30 ml) soy sauce
¼ teaspoon ground ginger
1 red capsicum, thinly sliced

- Preheat oven to 160° C (325° F).
- Brown chicken breasts in large frypan with oil. Place in sprayed 25 x 38-cm (10 x 15-inch) baking dish.
- Combine cornflour, sugar, brown sugar and stock powder in large saucepan and mix well.
- Drain pineapple and save juice. Add pineapple juice, orange juice, vinegar, ketchup, soy sauce and ginger to cornflour mixture in saucepan and mix well.
- Cook on high heat, stirring constantly, until mixture thickens. Pour sauce over chicken breasts.
- Bake for 45 minutes.
- Remove from oven, add pineapple chunks and thinly sliced capsicums and bake for an additional 15 minutes. Serves 12 to 14.

Corn-Chip Chicken

280 g (10 ounces) corn chips
1 onion, chopped
3 sticks celery, chopped
1 280-g (10-ounce) can cream of chicken soup
2 280-g (10-ounce) cans chopped tomatoes
100 g (3 ounces) green chillies, sliced
450 g (16 ounces) cubed cheddar cheese
4–5 boneless, skinless chicken breast halves, cooked, cubed

- Preheat oven to 175° C (350° F).
- Place half chips in sprayed 23 x 33-cm (9 x 13-inch) baking dish and crush a few chips with your hand.
- Combine onion, celery, chicken soup, tomatoes, green chillies and cheese in large saucepan. Stir on medium heat until cheese melts. Add chicken and pour over chips.
- Crush remaining chips in resealable plastic bag with rolling pin. Sprinkle over chicken-cheese mixture.
- Bake for about 35 minutes or until bubbly around edges. Serves 10.

Chicken-Run Casserole

1 onion, chopped
1 cup (100 g) sliced celery
3 tablespoons (45 g) butter
4 cups (460 g) diced cooked chicken
170 g (6 ounces) long-grain wild rice, cooked
1 280-g (10-ounce) can cream of celery soup
1 280-g (10-ounce) can cream of chicken soup
1 115-g (4-ounce) jar roasted red capsicum, drained
2 425-g (15-ounce) cans green beans, drained
1 cup (170 g) slivered almonds
1 cup (225 g) mayonnaise
2½ cups (140 g) crushed potato chips

- Preheat oven to 175° C (350° F).
- Sauté onion and celery in butter in large saucepan. Add chicken, rice, soups, capsicum, green beans, almonds, mayonnaise, ½ teaspoon salt and 1 teaspoon pepper and heat enough to mix.
- Pour into sprayed 25 x 38-cm (10 x 15-inch) baking dish. (This recipe needs a very large baking dish.)
- Sprinkle crushed potato chips over casserole and bake for 35 minutes or until potato chips are light brown. Serves 12 to 14.

Cheesy, Cheesy Chicken

Cheese lovers dig in!
This is a real winner.

1 onion, chopped
1 red capsicum, chopped
½ green capsicum, chopped
½ cup (115 g) butter
1 280-g (10-ounce) can cream of chicken soup
1 115-g (4-ounce) can sliced mushrooms
½ teaspoon dried coriander
½ teaspoon dried basil
1 teaspoon celery salt
½ teaspoon garlic pepper
230 g (8 ounces) egg noodles, cooked al dente and drained
4–5 boneless, skinless chicken breast halves, cooked, cubed
425 g (15 ounces) ricotta cheese
450 g (16 ounces) shredded cheddar cheese
⅓ cup (35 g) grated parmesan cheese
1 cup (60 g) breadcrumbs

- Preheat oven to 175° C (350° F).
- Sauté onion and capsicums with 5 tablespoons (75 g) butter in a frypan. Remove from heat and stir in soup, mushrooms, coriander, basil, celery salt, garlic pepper and a little salt.
- Combine noodles, chicken, cheeses and soup-mushroom mixture in large bowl. Mix well.
- Spoon into sprayed 23 x 33-cm (9 x 13-inch) baking dish.
- Melt 3 tablespoons (45 g) butter and combine with breadcrumbs in bowl. Sprinkle over casserole.
- Cover and bake for 45 minutes. Serves 10.

The Chicken Takes the Artichoke

6 boneless, skinless chicken breast halves
7 tablespoons (105 g) butter
1 400-g (14-ounce) jar water-packed artichoke hearts, drained
1 230-g (8-ounce) can sliced water chestnuts, drained
¼ cup (30 g) flour
⅛ teaspoon ground nutmeg
1 teaspoon dried thyme
400 ml (14 ounces) chicken stock
½ cup (125 ml) whipping cream
1 cup (110 g) shredded Swiss cheese
1 cup (120 g) seasoned breadcrumbs

- Preheat oven to 175° C (350° F).
- Brown chicken breasts in 2 tablespoons (30 g) butter in frypan. Place chicken breasts in sprayed 23 x 33-cm (9 x 13-inch) baking dish.
- Cut each artichoke heart in half and place artichokes and water chestnuts around chicken.
- Melt 3 tablespoons (45 g) butter in saucepan and stir in flour, ½ teaspoon pepper, nutmeg and thyme until smooth and mix well.
- Gradually stir in stock and cook on medium-high heat, stirring constantly, until stock thickens. Remove from heat and stir in cream and cheese.
- Blend until cheese melts and pour over chicken, artichokes and water chestnuts.
- Combine breadcrumbs and 2 tablespoons (30 g) melted butter in bowl and sprinkle over top of casserole. Bake for 35 minutes. Serves 8.

Three Cheers for Chicken

8 boneless, skinless chicken breast halves
6 tablespoons (85 g) butter
1 onion, chopped
½ green capsicum, chopped
1 115-g (4-ounce) jar chopped roasted red capsicum, drained
1 cup (95 g) rice
1 280-g (10-ounce) can cream of chicken soup
1 280-g (10-ounce) can cream of celery soup
1 230-g (8-ounce) can sliced water chestnuts
1 cup (115 g) shredded cheddar cheese

- Preheat oven to 175° C (350° F).
- Salt and pepper chicken and place in sprayed 25 x 38-cm (10 x 15-inch) glass baking dish.
- Melt butter in medium saucepan and add onion, capsicums, rice, soups, 2 soup cans of water and water chestnuts and pour over chicken.
- Cover and bake for 15 minutes, reduce temperature to 160° C (325° F) and cook for an additional 1 hour. Add cheese 5 minutes before dish is done and return to oven for last 5 minutes. Serves 12 to 14.

Tomato-Chicken Enchiladas

2 370-g (13-ounce) cans tomatoes, drained
1 200-g (7-ounce) jar chopped green chillies
Juice of ½ lemon
6 tablespoons (90 ml) canola oil
1 onion, chopped
1 clove garlic, minced
400 ml (14 ounces) chicken stock
12 corn tortillas
3 cups (420 g) shredded cooked chicken
340 g (12 ounces) shredded cheddar cheese, divided
230 g (8 ounces) sour cream

- Preheat oven to 175° C (350° F).
- Combine tomatoes, green chillies and lemon juice in blender and process. Heat 2 tablespoons (30 ml) oil with onion and garlic in large frypan and cook until onion is translucent.
- Stir in puree and chicken stock. Simmer until sauce reduces to consistency of tomato sauce.
- In separate frypan, heat remaining oil and cook tortillas about 3 seconds on each side. Dip softened tortilla into tomato mixture. Lay sauced tortilla on plate. Place ¼ cup (35 g) chicken and 2 tablespoons (15 g) cheese across tortilla and roll to close.
- Place enchilada, seam-side down, in 25 x 38-cm (10 x 15-inch) baking pan. Repeat until all tortillas are filled. Spoon remaining sauce over enchiladas.
- Cover and bake for about 35 minutes. Uncover, top with reserved cheese and bake for an additional 10 minutes. When ready to serve, top each enchilada with 1 spoonful sour cream. Serves 10.

Taco Casserole

1 280-g (10-ounce) can cream of mushroom soup
1 280-g (10-ounce) can cream of chicken soup
1 cup (250 ml) milk
1 30-g (1-ounce) packet taco seasoning
1 onion, chopped
1 115-g (4-ounce) jar chopped green chillies, drained
5–6 boneless, skinless chicken breast halves, cooked
1 455-g (16-ounce) bag corn chips
450 g (16 ounces) shredded cheddar cheese

- Preheat oven to 160° C (325° F).
- Combine soups, milk, taco seasoning, onion and green chillies in bowl. Cut chicken breasts into bite-size pieces.
- Layer one-half chips, half chicken, half soup mixture and half cheese in sprayed 23 x 33-cm (9 x 13-inch) glass dish. Repeat layers in same order. Cheese will be on top. Bake for 1 hour. Serves 8.

A chicken will lay bigger and stronger eggs if you change the lighting to make it think a day is 28 hours long.

Zesty Orange Chicken

½ cup (125 ml) white wine
½ cup (125 ml) orange juice
½ cup (160 g) orange marmalade
½ teaspoon ground ginger
½ teaspoon ground cinnamon
1 chicken, quartered
620 g (22 ounces) mandarin, peeled and sliced
½ cup (75 g) halved green grapes
1½ cups (280 g) instant brown rice, cooked

- Preheat oven to 160° C (325° F).
- Combine wine, orange juice, marmalade, ginger and cinnamon in sprayed 23 x 33-cm (9 x 13-inch) baking dish. Add chicken quarters and turn to coat chicken.
- Bake, basting occasionally for 40 minutes. Add mandarins and grapes to dish during last 5 minutes of cooking.
- Serve over brown rice. Serves 10.

Easy Chicken Casserole

1 cup (100 g) chopped celery
1 red capsicum, seeded and chopped
1 large onion, chopped
3 tablespoons (45 ml) olive oil
1–1.5 kg (2–3 pounds) chicken, cooked, chopped
230 g (8 ounces) macaroni, cooked, drained
1 280-g (10-ounce) can cream of mushroom soup
230 g (8 ounces) shredded cheddar cheese

- Preheat oven to 175° C (350° F).
- Sauté celery, red capsicum and onion in oil in a frypan. Combine remaining ingredients except 1 cup (100 g) cheese and mix well.
- Spoon into sprayed 23 x 33-cm (9 x 13-inch) baking dish. Top with remaining 1 cup (100 g) cheese. Bake for 20 minutes or until cheese melts.
Serves 6 to 8.

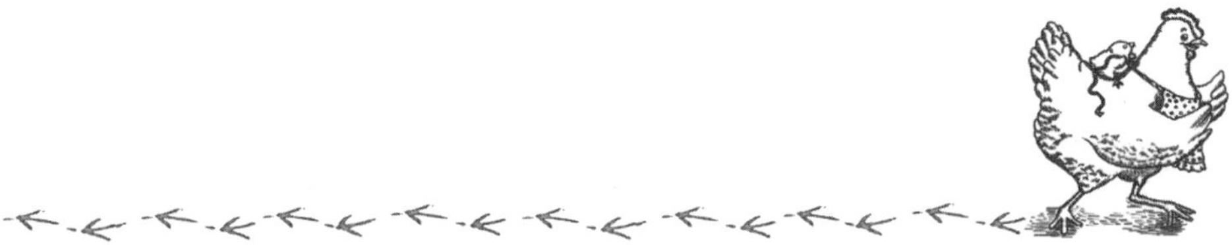

Adobe Chicken

2 cups (390 g) cooked brown rice
1 280-g (10-ounce) can chopped tomatoes, drained
60 g (2 ounces) green chillies, sliced
3 cups (420 g) cooked, chopped chicken
230 g (8 ounces) shredded cheddar cheese

- Preheat oven to 160° C (325° F).
- Combine rice, tomatoes, green chillies, chicken and half cheese.
- Spoon into sprayed 18 x 28-cm (7 x 11-inch) baking dish. Cover and bake for 30 minutes.
- Uncover, sprinkle with remaining cheese and return to oven for 5 minutes. Serves 6 to 8.

Gobble Gobble Casserole

1 200-g (7-ounce) package herb-seasoned stuffing
1 cup (280 g) cranberry sauce
340 g (12 ounces) cooked, chopped turkey
250 ml (8 ounces) chicken gravy

- Preheat oven to 190° C (375° F).
- Prepare stuffing according to package directions.
- Combine prepared stuffing and cranberry sauce in medium bowl and set aside.
- Place turkey in sprayed 2-L (2-quart) baking dish. Pour gravy over turkey and spoon stuffing mixture over casserole.
- Bake for 15 to 20 minutes. Serves 8.

Gobbler Supreme

1 onion, chopped
1 cup (100 g) sliced celery
3 tablespoons (45 g) butter
4 cups (560 g) cooked, diced turkey
170 g (6 ounces) long-grain and wild rice mix, cooked
1 teaspoon chicken stock powder
2 280-g (10-ounce) cans cream of chicken soup
1 115-g (4-ounce) jar roasted red capsicum, drained
2 425-g (15-ounce) cans green beans, drained
1 cup (170 g) slivered almonds
1 cup (225 g) mayonnaise
2½ cups (140 g) crushed potato chips

- Preheat oven to 175° C (350° F).
- Sauté onion and celery in butter in large saucepan.
- Add turkey, rice, stock powder, soup, roasted capsicum, green beans, almonds, mayonnaise, ½ teaspoon salt and 1 teaspoon pepper and stir.
- Pour into sprayed 25 x 38-cm (10 x 15-inch) baking dish. (This needs a very large casserole dish.) Sprinkle crushed potato chips over casserole.
- Bake for 35 minutes or until potato chips brown slightly. Serves 12.

TIP: If you want to make this dish in advance and freeze it, add the potato chips when you are ready to cook the casserole.

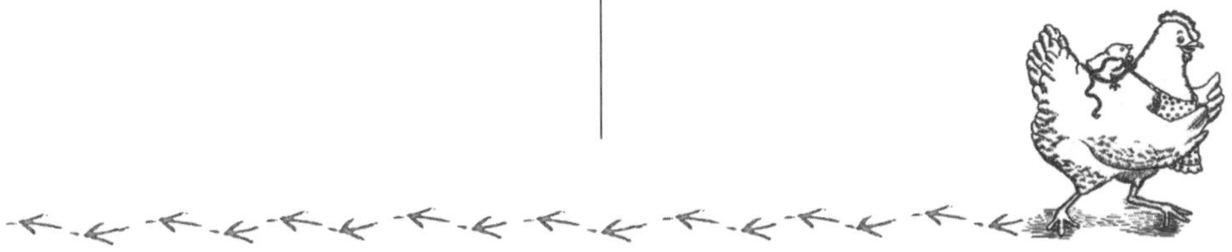

Turkey Perky Dinner

900 g (2 pounds) lemon-garlic seasoned turkey or chicken tenderloin
12–14 medium new (red) potatoes, halved
800 ml (27 ounces) chicken stock
½ cup (115 g) butter
5–6 medium yellow squash, sliced
¼ cup (30 g) cornflour

- Preheat oven to 160° C (325° F).
- Place turkey tenderloin in 23 x 33-cm (9 x 13-inch) baking dish lined with foil. Sprinkle lots of pepper over turkey and bake for 1 hour 30 minutes.
- After tenderloin has cooked for 1 hour 10 minutes, place new potatoes in large saucepan and add 400 ml chicken stock and ¼ cup (60 g) butter. Cook for 15 to 20 minutes or until tender.
- While potatoes cook, place squash in second saucepan and add remaining stock and butter. Cook for about 10 minutes or until squash is just barely tender.
- Place tenderloin on large platter and use slotted spoon to place potatoes and squash around sliced tenderloin.
- Combine cornflour and about ½ cup (125 ml) cooking stock and mix well. Combine stock into 1 saucepan, bring to boil and stir in cornflour mixture. Add about 1 teaspoon pepper (and salt if you like) and cook, stirring constantly until liquid thickens.
- Serve in gravy boat with tenderloin and vegetables. Serves 12.

Crispy Chicky Chicken

170 g (6 ounces) long-grain and wild rice mix, cooked
2 cups (200 g) chopped celery
1 onion, chopped
1 cup (130 g) coarsely chopped walnuts
2 tablespoons (30 g) butter
2 cups (450 g) mayonnaise
230 g (8 ounces) sour cream
1 tablespoon (15 ml) lemon juice
4 cups (560 g) cooked, cubed chicken
1 cup (55 g) crushed potato chips
85 g (3 ounces) onion, finely sliced and fried until crispy

- Preheat oven to 160° C (325° F).
- Lightly sauté celery, onion and walnuts in butter in frypan. Add mayonnaise, sour cream, lemon juice, ¾ teaspoon salt and chicken and mix well.
- Fold in cooked rice and transfer to sprayed 23 x 33-cm (9 x 13-inch) baking dish.
- Combine potato chips and onion in bowl and sprinkle over top of casserole.
- Bake for 25 minutes. Serves 10 to 12.

Tempting Chicken and Veggies

680 g (1½ pounds) chicken breast tenderloins
½ cup (115 g) butter
1 170-g (6-ounce) packet fried rice with seasoning packet
⅛ teaspoon cayenne pepper
¼ cup (40 g) chopped red capsicum
1 280-g (10-ounce) package frozen broccoli florets, thawed
1 280-g (10-ounce) package frozen corn, thawed

- Preheat oven to 175° C (350° F).
- Brown chicken tenderloins in about 3 tablespoons (45 g) butter in frypan. Remove chicken to large bowl.
- In same frypan, sauté rice until light brown with remaining butter and spoon into bowl with chicken. Add 2½ cups (625 ml) water, cayenne pepper, capsicum, broccoli and corn and mix well.
- Spoon into sprayed 23 x 33-cm (9 x 13-inch) baking dish. Cover and bake for 25 minutes or until rice and vegetables are tender. Serves 10.

A broody is a hen that has laid or contributed to a clutch of eggs and is now waiting for them to hatch.

Barnyard Bakes and Grills

From hearty to light, spicy to mild, these inventive chicken specialties will make you fly over the coop. Just combine these wonderful ingredients, put them in the oven – and stand back!

Barnyard Bakes and Grills Contents

Barnyard Bakes and Grills Contents

Apache Trail Drumsticks

⅔ cup (80 g) fine, dry breadcrumbs
⅔ cup (40 g) finely crushed corn chips
1 30-g (1-ounce) packet taco seasoning mix
1 455-g (16-ounce) jar taco sauce
900 g (2 pounds) chicken drumsticks, skinned

- Preheat oven to 190° C (375° F).
- Combine breadcrumbs, crushed corn chips and dry taco seasoning mix in bowl. Place ½ cup (135 g) taco sauce in flat bowl.
- Dip drumsticks in taco sauce, one at a time, then dredge in crumb mixture. Discard taco sauce used for dipping.
- Place drumsticks on sprayed 25 x 38-cm (10 x 15-inch) baking pan and bake for 30 to 35 minutes. Serve with remaining taco sauce. Serves 8.

Apricot-Ginger Chicken

2 teaspoons ground ginger
½ cup (125 ml) Italian dressing
4 boneless, skinless chicken breast halves
⅔ cup (210 g) apricot jam

- Combine ginger and Italian dressing and place in large resealable plastic bag. Add chicken to bag, marinate in refrigerator for 6–8 hours, turning occasionally.
- When ready to bake, preheat oven to 175° C (350° F). Remove chicken and reserve ¼ cup (60 ml) marinade. Place chicken in shallow baking dish.
- Pour ¼ cup (60 ml) marinade into a saucepan, bring to boil and cook for 1 minute. Remove from heat, stir in apricot jam and set aside.
- Bake for 45 minutes and brush with marinade mixture during last 10 minutes of cooking. Serves 4.

Aztec Creamy Salsa Chicken

6 boneless, skinless chicken breast halves
1 30-g (1-ounce) packet taco seasoning mix
1 455-g (16-ounce) jar salsa
230 g (8 ounces) sour cream

- Preheat oven to 175° C (350° F).
- Brown chicken in frypan and transfer to sprayed 23 x 33-cm (9 x 13-inch) baking dish. Sprinkle taco seasoning over chicken and top with salsa.
- Cover and bake for 35 minutes.
- Remove chicken to serving plates. Add sour cream to juices in pan, stir well and microwave on high for about 2 minutes. Stir pan juices and sour cream for sauce to serve over chicken. Serves 6.

Bacon-Wrapped Chicken

6 boneless, skinless chicken breast halves
230 g (8 ounces) cream cheese with onion and chives
Butter
6 bacon strips

- Preheat oven to 190° C (375° F).
- Flatten chicken to 1-cm (½-inch) thickness and spread 3 tablespoons (40 g) cream cheese over each piece.
- Dot with butter and sprinkle with a little salt; roll and wrap each with 1 bacon strip.
- Place seam-side down in sprayed 23 x 33-cm (9 x 13-inch) baking dish and bake for 40 to 45 minutes or until juices run clear.
- To brown, place 15 cm (6 inches) under griller for about 3 minutes or until bacon is crisp. Serves 6.

Baked Chicken Poupon

2 tablespoons (30 g) Dijon-style mustard
2 tablespoons (30 ml) oil
1 teaspoon garlic powder
½ teaspoon Italian seasoning
4 boneless, skinless chicken breast halves

- Preheat oven to 190° C (375° F).
- Mix mustard, oil, garlic powder and seasoning in resealable plastic bag, add chicken breasts and marinate for 15 minutes.
- Place chicken in sprayed 23 x 33-cm (9 x 13-inch) baking pan.
- Bake for 35 minutes. Serves 4.

Easy Baked Chicken

6 boneless, skinless chicken breast halves
½ cup (115 g) butter, melted
Stuffing mix with seasoning

- Preheat oven to 175° C (350° F).
- Dip chicken breasts in melted butter.
- Roll in stuffing mix to coat.
- Bake for 45 minutes. Serves 6.

Finger Lickin' BBQ Chicken

1 900-g (2-pound) chicken, quartered
½ cup (135 g) tomato sauce
¼ cup (60 g) butter, melted
2 tablespoons (25 g) sugar
1 tablespoon (15 g) mustard
½ teaspoon minced garlic
¼ cup (60 ml) lemon juice
¼ cup (60 ml) white vinegar
¼ cup (60 ml) Worcestershire sauce

- Preheat oven to 160° C (325° F).
- Sprinkle chicken quarters with a little salt and pepper and brown in frypan. Place in sprayed 23 x 33-cm (9 x 13-inch) baking pan.
- Combine ketchup, butter, sugar, mustard, garlic, lemon juice, vinegar and Worcestershire sauce in bowl. Pour over chicken, cover and bake for 50 minutes. Serves 4.

Best-Ever Turkey Loaf

900 g (2 pounds) minced turkey
1 170-g (6-ounce) package stuffing mix
1 teaspoon Italian seasoning
2 eggs, beaten
½ cup (135 g) tomato sauce

- Preheat oven to 175° C (350° F).
- Combine minced turkey, stuffing mix, seasoning, eggs and ¼ cup (70 g) tomato sauce in bowl and mix well.
- Shape meat into an oval loaf in centre of sprayed 23 x 33-cm (9 x 13-inch) baking dish.
- Spread remaining ¼ cup (70 g) sauce on top of loaf.
- Bake for 1 hour. Serves 8.

Catalina Chicken

6 boneless, skinless chicken breast halves
1 230-g (8-ounce) bottle Thousand Island dressing
1½ cups (90 g) crushed cracker crumbs

- Preheat oven to 175° C (350° F).
- Marinate chicken in dressing for 3 to 4 hours and discard marinade. Combine 1 teaspoon pepper with cracker crumbs.
- Dip each chicken breast in crumbs and place in sprayed 23 x 33-cm (9 x 13-inch) baking dish.
- Bake for 1 hour. Serves 6 to 8.

Cheesy Crusted Chicken

¾ cup (170 g) mayonnaise (not light)
½ cup (50 g) grated parmesan cheese
5–6 boneless, skinless chicken breast halves
1 cup (120 g) breadcrumbs with Italian seasoning

- Preheat oven to 190° C (375° F).
- Combine mayonnaise and cheese in bowl. Place chicken breasts on sheet of baking paper and spread mayonnaise-cheese mixture over chicken. Sprinkle heavily with dry breadcrumbs on both sides.
- Place chicken in sprayed 23 x 33-cm (9 x 13-inch) baking pan so pieces do not touch.
- Bake for 20 minutes (25 minutes if chicken pieces are fairly large). Chicken pieces can be sliced and placed on serving platter. Serves 6.

Chicken and Beef Collide

100 g (3½ ounces) beef jerky
6 strips bacon
6 boneless, skinless chicken breast halves
1 280-g (10-ounce) can cream of chicken soup

- Preheat oven to 160° C (325° F).
- Place beef jerky in sprayed 23 x 33-cm (9 x 13-inch) baking dish. Wrap bacon strip around each chicken breast and place over beef.
- Heat chicken soup and ¼ cup (60 ml) water in saucepan and pour over chicken.
- Cover and bake for 1 hour. Serves 6.

Chicken Crunch

4–6 boneless, skinless chicken breast halves
½ cup (125 ml) Italian salad dressing
½ cup (120 g) sour cream
2½ cups (70 g) crushed cornflakes

- Place chicken in resealable plastic bag and add salad dressing and sour cream. Seal and refrigerate 1 hour. Remove chicken from marinade and discard marinade.
- When ready to bake, preheat oven to 190° C (375° F).
- Dredge chicken in cornflakes and place in sprayed 23 x 33-cm (9 x 13-inch) baking dish.
- Bake for 45 minutes. Serves 4 to 6.

Parmesan Chicken Breasts

6 boneless, skinless chicken breast halves
1½ cups (180 g) dry breadcrumbs
½ cup (50 g) grated parmesan cheese
1 teaspoon dried basil
½ teaspoon garlic powder
230 g (8 ounces) sour cream

- Preheat oven to 160° C (325° F).
- Flatten chicken to 1 cm (½ inch) thick. Combine breadcrumbs, parmesan cheese, basil and garlic powder in shallow dish.
- Dip chicken in sour cream, coat with crumb mixture and place (so chicken breasts do not touch) in sprayed 25 x 38-cm (10 x 15-inch) baking dish.
- Bake for 50 to 60 minutes or until golden brown. Serves 6.

Chicken Diablo

6 boneless, skinless chicken breast halves
230 g (8 ounces) cream cheese, softened
1 455-g (16-ounce) jar salsa
2 teaspoons ground cumin
1 bunch spring onions with tops, chopped

- Preheat oven to 175° C (350° F).
- Pound chicken breasts to flatten. Beat cream cheese in bowl until smooth; add salsa, cumin and onions.
- Place heaped spoonful of cream cheese mixture on each chicken breast and roll. (There will be left-over cream cheese mixture.)
- Place in sprayed 18 x 28-cm (7 x 11-inch) baking dish. Spoon remaining cream cheese mixture over chicken rolls. Cover and bake for 30 minutes, uncover and continue cooking until chicken rolls are light brown. Serves 6.

Chicken Dipping

1½ cups (55 g) stuffing mix
¼ cup (60 ml) olive oil
4 boneless, skinless chicken breast halves
¼ cup (60 ml) honey
3 tablespoons (45 g) spicy brown mustard

- Preheat oven to 175° C (350° F).
- Place stuffing mix in resealable plastic bag and crush with rolling pin.
- Add oil to centre of 23 x 33-cm (9 x 13-inch) baking pan and spread around entire pan.
- Cut chicken breasts into 3 or 4 pieces, dip in stuffing mix and place in baking pan. Arrange chicken in pan so the pieces are not touching.
- Bake for 25 minutes. Remove from oven, turn pieces over and bake for an additional 15 minutes or until brown.
- Combine honey and mustard in bowl and mix well. Dip chicken in dipping sauce and enjoy. Serves 4.

Q: Why did the chicken cross the basketball court?

A: He heard the referee calling fowls.

Chicken Oriental

1 170-g (6-ounce) jar sweet-and-sour sauce
1 30-g (1-ounce) packet onion soup mix
1 455-g (16-ounce) jar cranberry sauce
6 boneless, skinless chicken breast halves

- Preheat oven to 160° C (325° F).
- Combine sweet-and-sour sauce, onion soup mix and cranberry sauce in bowl.
- Place chicken breasts in sprayed 23 x 33-cm (9 x 13-inch) shallow baking dish. Pour cranberry mixture over chicken breasts.
- Cover and bake for 30 minutes. Uncover and bake for an additional 25 minutes. Serves 6 to 8.

Chicken Parmigiana

1½ cups (180 g) scone mix
⅔ cup (70 g) grated parmesan cheese
6 boneless, skinless chicken breast halves
½ cup (115 g) butter, melted

- Preheat oven to 160° C (325° F).
- Combine scone mix and parmesan cheese in shallow bowl.
- Dip chicken pieces in butter and then in scone-cheese mixture.
- Place in sprayed 23 x 33-cm (9 x 13-inch) baking dish. Bake for 1 hour or until light brown. Serves 6 to 8.

Chicken Parmigiana and Spaghetti

1 400-g (14-ounce) package frozen, cooked chicken cutlets in breadcrumbs, thawed
1 795-g (28-ounce) jar spaghetti sauce
280 g (10 ounces) grated parmesan cheese
230 g (8 ounces) thin spaghetti, cooked

- Preheat oven to 190° C (375° F).
- Place cutlets in sprayed 23 x 33-cm (9 x 13-inch) baking dish and top each with about ¼ cup (65 g) spaghetti sauce and 1 heaped tablespoon (15 g) parmesan. Bake for 15 minutes.
- Place cooked pasta on serving platter and top with cutlets. Sprinkle remaining cheese over cutlets. Heat remaining spaghetti sauce and serve with chicken and spaghetti. Serves 8.

Apricot Chicken

1 cup (320 g) apricot jam
1 230-g (8-ounce) bottle Thousand Island dressing
1 30-g (1-ounce) packet onion soup mix
6 boneless, skinless chicken breast halves
Rice, cooked

- Preheat oven to 160° C (325° F).
- Combine apricot jam, dressing and soup mix in bowl.
- Place chicken breasts in sprayed 23 x 33-cm (9 x 13-inch) baking dish and pour apricot mixture over chicken.
- Bake for 1 hour 20 minutes. Serve over rice. Serves 6 to 8.

Chicken Breast Eden Isle

230 g (8 ounces) sour cream
85 g (3 ounces) cream cheese, softened
1 280-g (10-ounce) can cream of chicken soup
70 g (2½ ounces) beef jerky
6 boneless, skinless chicken breast halves
6 strips bacon
Rice, cooked

- Preheat oven to 160° C (325° F).
- Beat sour cream, cream cheese and soup in bowl. Line bottom of baking dish with beef jerky. Place chicken breasts, wrapped with bacon strips onto jerky.
- Spoon sour cream mixture over chicken. Cover and bake for 2 hours. Uncover last few minutes to brown. Serve over rice. Serves 6.

Chicken Pockets

85 g (3 ounces) cream cheese, softened
3 tablespoons (45 g) butter, softened
340 g (12 ounces) cooked, chopped chicken
2 tablespoons (30 ml) milk
1 tablespoon (5 g) chopped chives
1 packet filo pastry
Oil or melted butter
Parmesan cheese
Breadcrumbs

- Preheat oven to 175° C (350° F).
- Combine cream cheese with butter in bowl until smooth. Add chicken, milk and chives plus ⅛ teaspoon salt.
- Lay out 3 to 4 sheets of filo pastry, brushing each sheet with oil or melted butter (follow the instructions on the packet).
- Spoon ⅛ mixture into centre of pastry. Pull 4 corners up and twist together. Seal sides by pinching together. Repeat to make 8 parcels.
- Brush parcels with milk and sprinkle with parmesan cheese and breadcrumbs. Bake on baking sheet for 20 to 25 minutes. Serves 8.

Fruited Chicken

6 large boneless, skinless chicken breast halves
½ cup (115 g) butter, melted
⅔ cup (80 g) flour
Paprika
1 425-g (15-ounce) can chunky fruit salad with juice

- Preheat oven to 175° C (350° F).
- Dip chicken in butter and flour. Place in sprayed 23 x 33-cm (9 x 13-inch) baking dish. Sprinkle with a little salt, pepper and paprika.
- Bake for 45 minutes.
- Pour fruit and half juice over chicken. Bake for an additional 20 minutes. Serves 6.

Chicken Pot Pie

425 g (15 ounces) refrigerated shortcrust pastry
1 540-g (19-ounce) can cream of chicken soup
2 cups (280 g) cooked diced chicken breasts
1 280-g (10-ounce) package frozen mixed vegetables, thawed

- Preheat oven to 160° C (325° F).
- Line a 23-cm (9-inch) deep-dish pie pan with pastry. Fill with chicken soup, chicken and mixed vegetables. Gently stir to mix.
- Cover with second layer of pastry, fold edges under and crimp. With knife, cut 4 slits in centre of pastry. Bake for 1 hour 15 minutes or until crust is golden brown. Serves 8.

TIP: When you're too busy to cook chicken, get a roast chicken from the supermarket.

Chicken Quesadillas

3 boneless, skinless chicken breast halves, cubed
280 g (10 ounces) processed cheese spread
⅔ cup (175 g) chunky salsa
10 flour tortillas

- Preheat oven to 205° C (400° F).
- Cook chicken in frypan until juices evaporate and stir often. Add spread and salsa and heat thoroughly.
- Spread about ⅓ cup (75 ml) mixture on half tortilla to within 1 cm (½ inch) of edge. Moisten edge with water, fold over and seal. Place tortillas on 2 baking trays.
- Bake for 5 to 6 minutes. Serves 8.

Barnyard Dinner

5 boneless, skinless chicken breast halves
5 slices onion
5 potatoes, peeled and quartered
1 280-g (10-ounce) can cream of celery soup

- Preheat oven to 160° C (325° F).
- Place chicken breasts in sprayed 23 x 33-cm (9 x 13-inch) baking dish. Top chicken with onion slices and place potatoes around chicken.
- Heat soup with ¼ cup (60 ml) water in saucepan; just enough to pour soup over chicken and vegetables.
- Cover and bake for 1 hour 10 minutes. Serves 5.

Chicken Salsa

6 boneless, skinless chicken breast halves
1 tablespoon (15 g) cornflour
1 455-g (16-ounce) jar salsa
¾ cup (255 g) honey
½ cup (125 ml) light soy sauce
2 tablespoons (30 ml) oil
½ teaspoon dried ginger

- Wash each chicken piece and dry with paper towels.
- Combine salsa, honey, soy sauce, oil and ginger into a bowl and mix well. Pour 1½ cups (375 ml) marinade into resealable plastic bag, add chicken and refrigerate 2 to 3 hours. Cover and refrigerate remaining marinade.
- When ready to bake, preheat oven to 175° C (350° F). Place drained chicken (discard chicken marinade) in sprayed 23 x 33-cm (9 x 13-inch) baking dish. Top with remaining refrigerated marinade and bake for 25 to 30 minutes or until chicken juices run clear.
- Remove chicken and keep warm. Combine cornflour with 2 tablespoons (30 ml) water in small saucepan and stir in pan juices.
- Bring to a boil and cook for about 2 minutes, stirring constantly until it thickens.
- To serve, pour sauce over chicken. Serves 6.

Chicken Scarborough Fair

For best results, make early in the day and refrigerate, or prepare 1 hour before serving.

6 boneless, skinless chicken breast halves
½ cup (115 g) butter, softened, divided
3 slices mozzarella cheese
1 egg, beaten
½ cup (60 g) flour
1 cup (120 g) seasoned breadcrumbs
2 tablespoons (5 g) chopped parsley
¼ teaspoon dried sage
¼ teaspoon rosemary
¼ teaspoon thyme
½ cup (125 ml) dry white wine

- Flatten chicken breasts between sheets of baking paper and spread half of butter over each piece. Season with a little salt and pepper and place 1 slice cheese on each piece.
- Roll chicken with ends tucked in. Beat egg with 1 tablespoon (15 ml) water. Coat chicken lightly with flour, dip in egg and roll in breadcrumbs. Arrange rolls seam-side down in sprayed 18 x 28-cm (7 x 11-inch) baking dish and refrigerate for 1 hour.
- When ready to bake, preheat oven to 175° C (350° F).
- Remove from refrigerator, melt remaining butter and add parsley, sage, rosemary and thyme in saucepan. Cover and bake for 30 minutes and baste with butter mixture.
- Remove from oven and pour wine over chicken. Bake for an additional 20 minutes and baste with pan juices. Serves 6.

Chicken and Broccoli Bake

2 packets boil-in-the-bag white rice
230 g (8 ounces) cubed processed cheese
1 455-g (16-ounce) package frozen broccoli florets, thawed
3 cups (420 g) cooked, cubed chicken or turkey
1 cup (60 g) cracker crumbs or breadcrumbs

- Preheat oven to 160° C (325° F).
- Cook rice in large saucepan according to package directions. Stir in cheese and ¼ cup (60 ml) water; stir and mix until cheese melts.
- Cook broccoli according to package directions. Add broccoli and chicken to rice-cheese mixture and mix well.
- Spoon into sprayed 23 x 33-cm (9 x 13-inch) baking dish. Top with crumbs and bake for 15 minutes. Serves 8.

Chip Chicken

2 cups (110 g) crushed potato chips
¼ teaspoon garlic powder
5–6 boneless, skinless chicken breast halves
½ cup (115 g) butter, melted

- Preheat oven to 175° C (350° F).
- Combine potato chips and garlic powder in bowl and mix well.
- Dip chicken breasts in butter and roll in potato chip mixture.
- Place in sprayed shallow baking dish and bake for 55 minutes. Serves 6.

Chicken and Cheese Enchiladas

1 30-g (1-ounce) packet taco seasoning
2 tablespoons (30 ml) olive oil
4–5 large boneless, skinless chicken breast halves, cubed
1 455-g (16-ounce) jar chunky salsa, divided
340 g (12 ounces) shredded cheddar cheese
425 g (15 ounces) ricotta cheese
1 115-g (4-ounce) jar chopped green chillies
1 egg
1 teaspoon dried coriander
10 20-cm (8-inch) flour tortillas
Sour cream

- Combine ¼ cup (60 ml) water, taco seasoning and 1 tablespoon (15 ml) oil in shallow bowl and mix well. Place seasoning mixture in resealable plastic bag. Add chicken, seal and refrigerate for 1 to 2 hours.
- When ready to bake, preheat oven to 175° C (350° F).
- Cook chicken in remaining oil in frypan over medium-high heat for about 15 minutes.
- Combine ½ cup (65 g) salsa and ¼ cup (60 ml) water and spoon into sprayed 23 x 33-cm (9 x 13-inch) baking dish. Spread evenly over bottom of dish.
- Combine 2½ cups (285 g) cheddar cheese, ricotta cheese, green chillies, egg, coriander and ½ teaspoon salt in bowl.
- Spoon ⅓ cup (40 g) cheese mixture down centre of each tortilla, top with chicken and roll. Place tortillas seam-side down over salsa mixture in dish.
- Drizzle remaining salsa over enchiladas and sprinkle with remaining cheese.
- Bake for 25 minutes. To serve, top with a dab of sour cream. Serves 6 to 8.

Almond-Crusted Chicken

1 egg
¼ cup (30 g) seasoned breadcrumbs
1 cup (190 g) sliced almonds
4 boneless, skinless chicken breast halves
145 g (5 ounces) grated parmesan cheese
1 teaspoon minced garlic
⅓ cup (55 g) finely chopped onion
2 tablespoons (30 ml) oil
1 cup (250 ml) white wine
¼ cup (60 ml) teriyaki sauce

- Preheat oven to 160° C (325° F).
- Place egg and 1 teaspoon water in shallow bowl and beat.
- In separate shallow bowl, combine breadcrumbs and almonds. Dip each chicken breast in egg, then in almond mixture, and place in sprayed 23 x 33-cm (9 x 13-inch) baking pan.
- Bake for 20 minutes. Remove chicken from oven and sprinkle parmesan cheese over each breast. Bake for an additional 15 minutes or until almonds and cheese are golden brown.
- Sauté garlic and onion in oil in saucepan.
- Add wine and teriyaki sauce and bring to a boil. Reduce heat and simmer for about 10 minutes or until mixture reduces by half.
- When serving, divide sauce among 4 plates and place chicken breasts on top. Serves 4.

Chicken-Taco Bake

12 tortillas
Olive oil
1 onion, chopped
2 tablespoons (30 g) butter
2 cups (500 ml) tomato juice
1 115-g (4-ounce) jar chopped green chillies
340 g (12 ounces) shredded cheddar cheese
250 ml (8 ounces) whipping cream
5 boneless, skinless chicken breast halves, boiled and cubed

- Preheat oven to 175° C (350° F).
- Quarter tortillas and fry in oil in frypan until crisp. Drain and set aside.
- Sauté onion in butter in frypan, add tomato juice, ½ teaspoon each of salt and pepper and green chillies. Simmer for 30 minutes.
- Add cheese, cream and chicken and heat until cheese melts.
- Alternate layers of chicken-cheese mixture and tortillas in sprayed 23 x 33-cm (9 x 13-inch) baking dish.
- Bake for 30 to 35 minutes. Serves 8.

An egg starts growing into a chick when it reaches a temperature of 30 degrees.

Chilli-Chicken Roll-Ups

8 boneless, skinless chicken breast halves
2 115-g (4-ounce) jars diced green chillies
230 g (8 ounces) shredded cheddar cheese
½ cup (115 g) butter, melted
2 cups (110 g) crushed tortilla chips

- Place each chicken breast on baking paper, flatten to about ½ cm (¼ inch) thick with rolling pin or mallet and season with 1 teaspoon salt and ½ teaspoon pepper.
- Place green chillies and a little cheese evenly in centre of each chicken breast. Carefully roll each chicken breast so no chillies or cheese seep out and secure with toothpicks.
- Place chicken in small baking dish and refrigerate for several hours or overnight.
- When ready to bake, preheat oven to 175° C (350° F). Roll each chicken breast in melted butter and crushed tortilla chips.
- Bake for about 25 to 30 minutes or until tender. Serves 8.

Chilly Night Turkey Bake

1 170-g (6-ounce) package stuffing mix
680 g (1½ pounds) deli turkey
1 280-g (10-ounce) can cream of chicken soup
½ cup (120 g) sour cream
1 455-g (16-ounce) bag frozen mixed vegetables, thawed, drained

- Preheat oven to 190° C (375° F).
- Sprinkle ½ cup (20 g) dry stuffing mix evenly in sprayed 23 x 33-cm (9 x 13-inch) baking dish. Set aside.
- Combine remaining stuffing and 1 cup (250 ml) water in bowl and stir just until moist. Set aside.
- Slice turkey into 2-cm (1-inch) strips and place over dry stuffing mix in baking dish. Mix soup, sour cream and vegetables in bowl, spoon over turkey strips and top with prepared stuffing. Bake for 25 minutes. Serves 8.

At the supermarket, select red meat and poultry last so they stay chilled.

Lemon-Chicken Breeze

4–6 frozen, boneless, skinless chicken breast halves
½ cup (115 g) butter
2–3 tablespoons (30–45 ml) oil
2–3 tablespoons (15–25 ml) flour
½ cup (125 ml) dry white wine
¼ cup (60 ml) lemon juice
4 tablespoons (8 g) chopped parsley

- Preheat oven to 175°C (350° F).
- While chicken is slightly frozen, slice each breast into 3 thin slices. Melt butter in frypan with oil, dredge chicken in flour and brown on all sides. Drain chicken on paper towels.
- Add wine, lemon juice, parsley and a little salt and pepper to frypan and mix.
- Place chicken breasts in sprayed 23 x 33-cm (9 x 13-inch) baking dish and pour lemon mixture over chicken.
- Bake for 15 minutes or until sauce seeps into chicken. Serves 4 to 6.

Snazzy Chicken

4 boneless, skinless chicken breast halves
¼ cup (60 ml) lime juice
30 ml (1 ounce) Italian salad dressing
¼ cup (60 g) butter, melted

- Preheat oven to 160° C (325° F).
- Season chicken with a little salt and pepper and place in sprayed 18 x 28-cm (7 x 11-inch) baking dish.
- Mix lime juice, salad dressing and melted butter in bowl and pour over chicken.
- Cover and bake for 1 hour. Remove cover for last 15 minutes of cooking time. Serves 4.

Cola Chicken

4–6 boneless, skinless chicken breast halves
1 cup (270 g) tomato sauce
1 cup (250 ml) cola
2 tablespoons (30 ml) Worcestershire sauce

- Preheat oven to 175° C (350° F).
- Place chicken in sprayed 23 x 33-cm (9 x 13-inch) baking dish and sprinkle with a little salt and pepper.
- Mix tomato sauce, cola and Worcestershire sauce in bowl and pour over chicken.
- Cover and bake for 50 minutes. Serves 6.

Coriander Chicken Breasts

6 boneless, skinless chicken breast halves
3 teaspoons snipped coriander
1¼ teaspoons ground cumin
2 cups (120 g) breadcrumbs
Olive oil
3 tablespoons (45 g) butter
¼ cup (30 g) flour
2 cups (500 ml) milk
⅓ cup (85 ml) dry white wine
230 g (8 ounces) shredded cheddar cheese

- Preheat oven to 175° C (350° F).
- Pound chicken breast halves to ½ cm (¼ inch) thick with mallet or rolling pin.
- Mix 1 teaspoon each of salt and pepper, 2 teaspoons coriander and 1 teaspoon cumin. Sprinkle seasonings over chicken cutlets and dip cutlets in breadcrumbs.
- Heat oil in large frypan and brown chicken on both sides. Remove to sprayed 23 x 33-cm (9 x 13-inch) baking dish.
- Melt butter in saucepan, blend in flour, ½ teaspoon salt, 1 teaspoon coriander and ¼ teaspoon cumin in saucepan. Add milk, stir constantly and cook until sauce thickens.
- Remove from heat and stir in wine. Pour sauce over chicken. Cover and bake for 45 minutes.
- Remove from oven, sprinkle cheese on top of each piece of chicken and return to oven for 5 minutes. Serves 6.

Chilli-Pepper Chicken

5 boneless, skinless chicken breast halves
1 30-g (1-ounce) packet hot-and-spicy coating mixture
1 115-g (4-ounce) jar chopped green chillies
Chunky salsa

- Preheat oven to 190° C (375° F).
- Dredge chicken in coating mixture and place in sprayed 23 x 33-cm (9 x 13-inch) baking dish.
- Bake for 25 minutes.
- Remove from oven, spread green chillies over chicken breasts and return to oven for 5 minutes. Serve with salsa over each chicken breast. Serves 5.

Company's Coming Chicken

2 chickens, quartered
2 280-g (10-ounce) cans cream of mushroom soup
455 g (1 pint) sour cream
1 cup (250 ml) sherry
Rice, cooked

- Preheat oven to 150° C (300° F).
- Place chicken in large shallow baking dish.
- Combine soup, sour cream and sherry in saucepan. Pour mixture over chicken.
- Cover and bake for 1 hour 15 minutes. Serve over rice. Serves 8 to 10.

TIP: A little paprika on top makes this dish look great.

Cranberry-Glazed Quails

6 quails, thawed
1 455-g (16-ounce) jar whole berry cranberry sauce
¼ cup (60 g) butter
¼ cup (60 ml) orange juice
2 teaspoons grated orange peel

- Preheat oven to 190° C (375° F).
- Wash quails and pat dry with paper towels. Season inside and out with a little salt and pepper. Place quails in shallow pan without rack and bake for 15 minutes.
- Heat cranberry sauce, butter, orange juice and orange peel in saucepan. Pour mixture over quails.
- Lower temperature to 160° C (325° F) and continue to bake for an additional 15–20 minutes. Baste often with cranberry sauce until it browns well. Serves 6.

Creamy Chicken Bake

1 230-g (8-ounce) package pasta
1 455-g (16-ounce) package frozen broccoli florets, thawed and trimmed
¼ cup (60 g) butter, melted
230 g (8 ounces) shredded cheddar cheese
1 280-g (10-ounce) can cream of chicken soup
1 cup (250 ml) unthickened cream
¼ teaspoon ground mustard
3 cups (420 g) cooked, cubed chicken breasts
⅔ cup (110 g) slivered almonds

- Preheat oven to 160° C (325° F).
- Cook pasta according to package directions, drain and keep warm.
- Combine pasta and broccoli in large bowl. Add butter and cheese and stir until cheese melts.
- Stir in chicken soup, cream, mustard, chicken and 1 teaspoon each of salt and pepper. Spoon into sprayed 3-L (3-quart) baking dish.
- Cover and bake for about 25 minutes. Remove from oven, sprinkle with slivered almonds and cook for an additional 15 minutes. Serves 10.

Creamy Turkey Enchiladas

1 onion, finely chopped
3 spring onions with tops, chopped
2 tablespoons (30 g) butter
½ teaspoon garlic powder
1 200-g (7-ounce) jar chopped green chillies, drained
450 g (16 ounces) cream cheese, softened
3 cups (420 g) cooked, diced turkey or chicken
8 20-cm (8-inch) flour tortillas
500 ml (16 ounces) pouring cream
450 g (16 ounces) shredded cheddar cheese

- Preheat oven to 175° C (350° F).
- Sauté onion and spring onions in butter in large frypan.
- Add garlic powder, ½ teaspoon salt and green chillies and stir in cream cheese. Heat, stir until cream cheese melts and add diced turkey.
- Lay out 8 tortillas and spoon about 3 heaped tablespoons (50 ml) turkey mixture on each tortilla. Roll tortillas and place seam-side down in sprayed 23 x 33-cm (9 x 13-inch) baking dish.
- Pour cream over enchiladas and sprinkle cheese over enchiladas. Bake for 35 minutes. Serves 8.

Crispy Herb-Seasoned Chicken

2 cups (500 ml) buttermilk*
1.1–1.4 kg (2½–3 pounds) chicken, cut into quarters
1 255-g (9-ounce) package herb-seasoned stuffing mix
¼ cup (25 g) grated parmesan cheese
½ teaspoon cayenne pepper
½ cup (115 g) butter, melted

- Place buttermilk in large plastic container with lid and add chicken quarters. Turn several times to coat.
- Marinate in buttermilk in refrigerator for 8 hours. Discard marinade.
- Preheat oven to 175° C (350° F).
- Process stuffing mix, parmesan cheese and cayenne pepper in food processor until they blend well.
- Dip chicken pieces in melted butter and roll in stuffing mixture until they coat well.
- Place chicken on sprayed 23 x 33-cm (9 x 13-inch) baking tray and bake for 1 hour 10 minutes. Serves 6 to 8.

**TIP: To make buttermilk, mix 1 cup (250 ml) milk with 1 tablespoon (15 ml) lemon juice or vinegar and let milk rest for about 10 minutes.*

Cranberry Chicken

6 boneless, skinless chicken breast halves
1 455-g (16-ounce) jar whole-berry cranberry sauce
1 large tart apple, peeled, chopped
⅓ cup (45 g) chopped walnuts
1 teaspoon curry powder

- Preheat oven to 175° C (350° F).
- Place chicken in sprayed 23 x 33-cm (9 x 13-inch) baking pan and bake for 20 minutes.
- Combine cranberry sauce, apple, walnuts and curry powder in bowl and spoon over chicken.
- Bake for an additional 25 minutes or until chicken juices run clear. Serves 6.

Crispy Nutty Chicken

⅓ cup (50 g) minced dry-roasted peanuts
1 cup (30 g) cornflake crumbs
½ cup (125 ml) ranch-style buttermilk salad dressing
6 boneless, skinless chicken breast halves

- Preheat oven to 175° C (350° F).
- Combine peanuts and cornflake crumbs on baking paper. Pour dressing into pie dish, dip each piece of chicken in dressing and roll chicken in crumb mixture to coat.
- Arrange chicken in sprayed 23 x 33-cm (9 x 13-inch) baking dish. Bake for 50 minutes or until light brown. Serves 6.

Glazed Drumsticks

570 g (20 ounces) frozen chicken drumsticks
½ cup (125 ml) hoisin sauce
2 tablespoons (30 ml) light soy sauce
1 teaspoon minced garlic

- Preheat griller. Place drumsticks in a single layer in sprayed 23 x 33-cm (9 x 13-inch) baking dish and grill for 10 minutes. Turn drumsticks and grill for an additional 10 minutes.
- Preheat oven to 160° C (325° F).
- Combine hoisin sauce, soy sauce and garlic in bowl and mix well. Brush chicken drumsticks lightly with sauce and bake for 25 minutes.
- During baking time, remove from oven and brush with remaining sauce. Continue cooking until glaze bubbles and browns. Serves 8.

Easy Chicken

6 boneless, skinless chicken breast halves
1 280-g (10-ounce) can cream of chicken soup
85 g (3 ounces) cream cheese
230 g (8 ounces) sour cream
Lemon pepper
2 cups (330 g) instant rice, cooked

- Preheat oven to 150° C (300° F).
- Place chicken breasts in shallow 23 x 33-cm (9 x 13-inch) baking dish.
- Combine soup, cream cheese and sour cream in saucepan and heat on low just until cream cheese melts and ingredients mix well.
- Pour soup mixture over chicken breasts and sprinkle with lemon pepper. Cover and bake for 1 hour.
- Uncover, bake for an additional 15 minutes and serve over rice. Serves 8.

Curry-Glazed Chicken

3 tablespoons (45 g) butter
⅓ cup (115 g) honey
2 tablespoons (30 g) Dijon-style mustard
1½ teaspoons curry powder
4 boneless, skinless chicken breast halves
2 cups (330 g) instant rice, cooked

- Preheat oven to 190° C (375° F).
- Melt butter in 23 x 33-cm (9 x 13-inch) baking dish.
- Mix honey, mustard and curry powder in dish with butter.
- Add chicken to dish and turn until chicken coats with butter mixture.
- Bake for 50 minutes, baste twice and serve over rice. Serves 4.

Easy Oven Chicken

One step does it all!

6 tablespoons (85 g) butter
1 cup (95 g) rice
1 30-g (1-ounce) packet onion soup mix
1 cup (100 g) chopped celery
400 ml (14 ounces) chicken stock
1 280-g (10-ounce) can cream of chicken soup
8 boneless, skinless chicken breast halves

- Preheat oven to 160° C (325° F).
- Melt butter in 23 x 33-cm (9 x 13-inch) glass baking dish. Add all remaining ingredients, except chicken and 2 cups (500 ml) water.
- Lay chicken breasts in rice and liquid mixture and cover with foil. Bake for 1 hour 10 minutes. Serves 5.

Il Pronto Chicken

⅔ cup (80 g) seasoned breadcrumbs
½ cup (50 g) grated parmesan cheese
½ teaspoon garlic powder
4 boneless, skinless chicken breast halves
½ cup (115 g) butter, melted
Rice, cooked

- Preheat oven to 175° C (350° F).
- Combine breadcrumbs and cheese with garlic powder, and salt and pepper in bowl and mix well.
- Dip chicken in butter, roll in breadcrumb mixture and place in sprayed 23 x 33-cm (9 x 13-inch) baking dish.
- Cover and bake for 55 minutes. Serve over rice. Serves 4.

Elegant Chicken

3 cups (420 g) cooked shredded chicken
170 g (6 ounces) mixed long-grain and wild rice, cooked
1 280-g (10-ounce) can cream of celery soup
1 115-g (4-ounce) jar roasted red capsicum
1 cup (225 g) mayonnaise
1 425-g (15-ounce) can green beans, drained
85 g (3 ounces) onion, finely chopped and fried until crispy

- Preheat oven to 175° C (350° F).
- Combine all ingredients in bowl except onion.
- Pour into sprayed 3-L (3-quart) baking dish. Bake for 15 to 20 minutes.
- Top with fried onion and cook for an additional 10 minutes. Serves 12.

Family-Secret Chicken and Noodles

This is a great recipe to prepare beforehand and freeze.

¼ cup (60 g) butter
½ cup (60 g) flour
½ teaspoon basil
½ teaspoon parsley
2 cups (500 ml) milk
1 115-g (4-ounce) can sliced mushrooms, drained
1 280-g (10-ounce) can cream of mushroom soup
1 60-g (2-ounce) jar diced roasted red capsicum
900 g (2 pounds) boneless, skinless chicken breast halves, cooked and diced
400 ml (14 ounces) chicken stock
1 455-g (16-ounce) package medium egg noodles
1 cup (115 g) shredded cheddar or mozzarella cheese

- Melt butter in saucepan over medium heat and add flour, seasonings and ½ teaspoon salt. Add milk slowly and stir constantly until thick.
- Add mushrooms, mushroom soup, capsicum, diced chicken and chicken stock. Cook noodles according to package directions. Drain.
- Mix noodles with sauce and stir gently. Pour mixture into 25 x 38-cm (10 x 15-inch) baking dish. Sprinkle with cheese, cover and refrigerate until baking time.
- When ready to bake, preheat oven to 175° C (350° F).
- Bake for 20 to 30 minutes until it heats thoroughly. Serves 12 to 14.

Happy Chicken Bake

6 boneless, skinless chicken breast halves
1 230-g (8-ounce) bottle Thousand Island dressing
1 30-g (1-ounce) packet onion soup mix
1 340-g (12-ounce) jar apricot jam
1 tablespoon (15 ml) lime juice
Rice, cooked

- Preheat oven to 160° C (325° F).
- Place chicken breasts in sprayed 23 x 33-cm (9 x 13-inch) baking dish.
- Combine dressing, soup mix, apricot jam and lime juice in saucepan. Heat just enough to mix.
- Pour over chicken breasts. Cover and bake for 1 hour 10 minutes. Serve over rice. Serves 8.

Flaky Chicken

8 boneless, skinless chicken breast halves
¾ cup (170 g) mayonnaise
2 cups (55 g) crushed cornflakes
½ cup (50 g) grated parmesan cheese

- Preheat oven to 160° C (325° F).
- Sprinkle chicken with a little salt and pepper. Dip chicken in mayonnaise and spread mayonnaise over chicken with brush.
- Combine cornflake crumbs and cheese in bowl and dip chicken in cornflake mixture until it completely coats chicken.
- Place chicken in sprayed 23 x 33-cm (9 x 13-inch) glass baking dish and bake for 1 hour. Serves 8.

Fiesta Chicken

½ cup (115 g) butter
2 cups (120 g) finely crushed cheese crackers
1 30-g (1-ounce) packet taco seasoning mix
5–6 boneless, skinless chicken breast halves, flattened
1 bunch spring onions with tops, chopped
1 teaspoon chicken stock powder
500 ml (1 pint) pouring cream
230 g (8 ounces) shredded cheddar cheese
1 115-g (4-ounce) jar chopped green chillies

- Preheat oven to 175° C (350° F).
- Melt butter in large baking dish and set aside. Combine cracker crumbs and taco mix in bowl. Dredge chicken in crumb mixture and pat mixture well to use all cracker crumbs.
- Place chicken in sprayed 23 x 33-cm (9 x 13-inch) baking dish with melted butter. Take out several tablespoons melted butter and place in saucepan. Add spring onions and sauté.
- Turn heat off, add chicken stock and stir. Add pouring cream, cheese, chopped green chillies and mix well. Pour over chicken in baking dish.
- Bake for 55 minutes. Serves 6.

Golden Chicken

6 boneless, skinless chicken breast halves
¼ cup (60 g) butter
1 280-g (10-ounce) can mushroom soup
½ cup (95 g) sliced almonds
½ teaspoon beef stock powder

- Preheat oven to 175° C (350° F).
- Place chicken breasts in sprayed 23 x 33-cm (9 x 13-inch) baking pan.
- Combine butter, soup, almonds, stock powder and ¼ cup (60 ml) water in saucepan. Heat and mix just until butter melts. Pour mixture over chicken.
- Cover and bake for 1 hour. Serves 6.

Four-Legged Chicken

4 boneless, skinless chicken breast halves
4 boneless, skinless thighs
4 skinless drumsticks
¾ cup (255 g) honey
½ cup (125 g) mustard
½ cup (115 g) butter, melted
1 teaspoon curry powder
1 teaspoon minced coriander

- Preheat oven to 175° C (350° F).
- Arrange all chicken pieces in sprayed 25 x 38-cm (10 x 15-inch) baking dish. Mix honey, mustard, butter, 1 teaspoon salt, curry powder and coriander in bowl. Spread evenly over chicken pieces.
- Bake for 30 minutes, remove from oven and baste chicken with pan juices. Return to oven and bake for an additional 30 minutes or until chicken is golden brown. Serves 8.

Ginger Orange-Glazed Quails

1 cup (250 ml) fresh orange juice
2 tablespoons (30 ml) plus ½ teaspoon peeled, minced fresh ginger
1 tablespoon (15 ml) soy sauce
3 tablespoons (30 g) honey
4 quails, halved

- Preheat oven to 205° C (400° F).
- Combine orange juice, 2 tablespoons (25 g) minced ginger, soy sauce and honey in saucepan and cook on high heat, stirring constantly for 3 minutes or until thick and glossy.
- Place quails in sprayed 23 x 33-cm (9 x 13-inch) baking dish and sprinkle ½ teaspoon ginger and ½ teaspoon each of salt and pepper over birds.
- Spoon glaze mixture over quails and bake for 20–25 minutes. Brush glaze over birds several times during cooking. Serves 2 to 4.

Creamy Chicken Soup

6–8 boneless, skinless chicken breast halves
1 280-g (10-ounce) can mushroom soup
½ teaspoon beef stock powder
1 cup (250 ml) white wine or white cooking wine
230 g (8 ounces) sour cream
Rice, cooked

- Preheat oven to 175° C (350° F).
- Place chicken breasts in sprayed 23 x 33-cm (9 x 13-inch) baking dish, sprinkle with a little salt and pepper and bake for 30 minutes.
- Combine soup, stock powder, wine and sour cream in saucepan and heat enough to mix well.
- Remove chicken from oven and cover with sour cream mixture.
- Reduce heat to 150° C (300° F) and return to oven for an additional 30 minutes. Baste twice. Serve over rice. Serves 8.

Honey-Baked Chicken

2 whole chickens, quartered
½ cup (115 g) butter, melted
⅔ cup (230 g) honey
¼ cup (60 g) Dijon-style mustard
1 teaspoon curry powder

- Preheat oven to 175° C (350° F).
- Place chicken pieces skin-side up in large, shallow baking dish and sprinkle with a little salt.
- Combine butter, honey, mustard and curry powder in bowl and pour over chicken.
- Bake for 1 hour 5 minutes and baste every 20 minutes. Serves 8.

Honey-Mustard Chicken

⅓ cup (85 g) Dijon-style mustard
½ cup (170 g) honey
2 tablespoons (4 g) dried dill
4 chicken quarters

- Preheat oven to 175° C (350° F).
- Combine mustard, honey and dill in bowl. Arrange chicken quarters in sprayed 23 x 33-cm (9 x 13-inch) baking dish.
- Pour mustard mixture over chicken. Turn chicken over and make sure mustard mixture covers chicken.
- Cover and bake for 35 minutes. Uncover and bake for an additional 10 minutes. Serves 4 to 6.

Lemonade Chicken

6 boneless, skinless chicken breast halves
170 ml (6 ounces) lemonade
⅓ cup (85 ml) soy sauce
1 teaspoon garlic powder

- Preheat oven to 175° C (350° F).
- Place chicken in sprayed 23 x 33-cm (9 x 13-inch) baking dish.
- Combine lemonade, soy sauce and garlic powder in bowl and pour over chicken.
- Cover and bake for 45 minutes. Uncover, pour juices over chicken and cook for an additional 10 minutes. Serves 4.

Oregano Chicken

¼ cup (60 g) butter, melted
10 g (½ ounce) Italian seasoning
2 tablespoons (30 ml) lemon juice
4 boneless, skinless chicken breast halves
2 tablespoons (5 g) dried oregano

- Preheat oven to 175° C (350° F).
- Combine butter, salad dressing mix and lemon juice in bowl. Place chicken in 23 x 33-cm (9 x 13-inch) baking pan and spoon butter mixture over chicken.
- Cover and bake for 45 minutes. Uncover, baste with pan drippings and sprinkle with oregano. Bake for an additional 15 minutes or until chicken juices run clear. Serves 4.

Herb-Roasted Turkey

2 tablespoons (20 g) poultry seasoning
2 teaspoons paprika
2 teaspoons garlic powder
½ teaspoon ground nutmeg
1 5.4-kg (12-pound) turkey, thawed
1 large onion, cut in wedges
2 tablespoons (30 ml) oil
1 30-g (1-ounce) packet chicken gravy mix
3 tablespoons (20 g) flour
1 cup (250 ml) pan drippings or chicken stock

- Preheat oven to 175° C (325° F).
- Combine poultry seasonings, paprika, garlic powder and ground nutmeg with 2 tablespoons (30 g) salt and 1 teaspoon pepper in small bowl to make a dry rub.
- Rinse turkey under cold water and pat dry. Place onion wedges in turkey cavity and rub about half of rub ingredients inside.
- Place turkey breast-side up on shallow roasting pan lined with heavy foil. Spread oil over outside of turkey. Sprinkle remaining rub mixture over outside and add ½ cup (125 ml) water to roasting pan.
- Cover loosely with heavy foil and bake for about 3 hours 30 minutes or until meat thermometer inserted in breast reaches 80° C (175° F). Let stand for about 15 minutes before carving. Reserve pan juices for gravy.
- Combine gravy mix and flour in saucepan. Slowly stir in pan drippings and 1 cup (250 ml) water, stirring constantly.
- Bring to a boil, reduce heat and stir constantly until mixture thickens. Serves 16 to 20.

Home-Style Chicken

2 cups (120 g) fine breadcrumbs
1 tablespoon (15 g) cumin
2 teaspoons chilli powder
½ teaspoon oregano
4 eggs
½ cup (130 g) prepared chilli salsa
2 cloves garlic, minced
3 tablespoons (45 g) butter
1.4–1.8 kg (3–4 pounds) boneless, skinless chicken breast halves
Iceberg lettuce
Sour cream
1 avocado
1 lime
Spring onions with tops, chopped

- Preheat oven to 175° C (350° F).
- Combine breadcrumbs, cumin, chilli powder, ½ teaspoon salt and oregano in large, shallow bowl and set aside. In separate bowl, beat eggs with salsa and garlic.
- Melt butter in 23 x 33-cm (9 x 13-inch) baking dish in oven. Dip chicken pieces into egg bowl and coat with breadcrumb mixture. Place pieces in baking dish and turn each piece in butter. Bake for about 35 to 40 minutes or until chicken is done.
- Place several leaves of iceberg lettuce on plate and serve chicken on top. Garnish with sour cream, avocado slices, lime slices and chopped spring onion. Serves 4.

Lemon-Almond Chicken

Asparagus, lemon juice, curry powder and almonds give a flavourful twist to an otherwise ordinary chicken dish.

2 425-g (15-ounce) cans cut asparagus, well drained
4 boneless, skinless chicken breast halves
3 tablespoons (45 g) butter
1 280-g (10-ounce) can cream of asparagus soup
⅔ cup (150 g) mayonnaise
¼ cup (60 ml) milk
1 red capsicum, cut in strips
2 tablespoons (30 ml) lemon juice
1 teaspoon curry powder
¼ teaspoon ground ginger
½ cup (95 g) sliced almonds, toasted

- Preheat oven to 175° C (350° F).
- Place asparagus in sprayed 18 x 28-cm (7 x 11-inch) baking dish and set aside. Sprinkle chicken with ½ teaspoon salt. Sauté chicken in butter in large frypan for about 15 minutes and cut into strips.
- Spoon chicken over asparagus. Combine asparagus soup, mayonnaise, milk, capsicum, lemon juice, curry powder, ginger and ¼ teaspoon pepper in frypan and heat just enough to mix well.
- Spoon over chicken and sprinkle almonds over top of casserole. Bake for 35 minutes. Serves 8 to 10.

Lemon-Herb Chicken

6 boneless, skinless chicken breast halves
1 cup (230 g) butter, melted, divided
1 cup (120 g) flour
¼ cup (60 ml) lemon juice
½ teaspoon lemon pepper
½ teaspoon garlic powder
2 tablespoons (30 g) brown sugar
½ teaspoon oregano
½ teaspoon crushed rosemary
1 teaspoon lemon peel
White rice, cooked

- Preheat oven to 175° C (350° F).
- Dip each chicken breast in butter and flour and place in sprayed 23 x 33-cm (9 x 13-inch) baking dish. Cover and bake for 30 minutes.
- While chicken is cooking, add lemon juice, lemon pepper, garlic, brown sugar, oregano, rosemary and lemon peel into a mixing bowl with remaining butter, ½ teaspoon salt and ¼ cup (60 ml) hot water and mix well.
- After chicken cooks for 30 minutes, uncover and pour lemon-herb sauce over chicken. Bake for an additional 25 minutes and serve over rice. Serves 5.

Montezuma Celebration Chicken

6 boneless, skinless chicken breast halves
1 jalapeno chilli, seeded and cut into rings
455 g (16 ounces) hot salsa
⅔ cup (150 g) packed brown sugar
1 tablespoon (15 g) spicy mustard
Envelope taco seasoning mix

- Preheat oven to 175° C (350° F).
- Place chicken breasts covered with jalapeno chilli rings in sprayed 23 x 33-cm (9 x 13-inch) baking dish without breasts touching each other. Combine salsa, brown sugar, mustard, taco seasoning and ½ teaspoon salt in bowl and spoon over each piece of chicken.
- Cover and bake for 35 to 40 minutes. Uncover and continue cooking for additional 10 to 15 minutes to let chicken breasts brown slightly. Serves 6.

TIP: For a less spicy Celebration Chicken, refer to p. 167.

A pip is the first small hole pecked through the eggshell as a chick gets ready to hatch.

Celebration Chicken

6 boneless, skinless chicken breast halves
1 onion, sliced
1 green capsicum, seeded and cut into rings
455 g (16 ounces) pasta sauce
⅔ cup (150 g) packed brown sugar
1 tablespoon (15 g) mustard

- Preheat oven to 175° C (350° F).
- Place chicken breasts covered with capsicum rings in sprayed 23 x 33-cm (9 x 13-inch) baking dish without breasts touching each other. Mix sauce, onion, brown sugar, mustard and ½ teaspoon salt in bowl and spoon over each piece of chicken.
- Cover and bake for 35 to 40 minutes. Uncover and continue cooking for additional 10 to 15 minutes to let chicken breasts brown slightly.

Mozzarella Chicken

4 boneless, skinless chicken breast halves
1 cup (120 g) dry Italian-seasoned breadcrumbs
1 cup (250 g) prepared spaghetti sauce
4 slices mozzarella cheese

- Preheat oven to 175° C (350° F).
- Pound each chicken breast to flatten slightly. Coat chicken well in breadcrumbs and arrange in sprayed 23 x 33-cm (9 x 13-inch) baking dish.
- Spread quarter of sauce over each portion. Place 1 slice cheese over each and garnish with remaining breadcrumbs. Bake for 45 minutes. Serves 4.

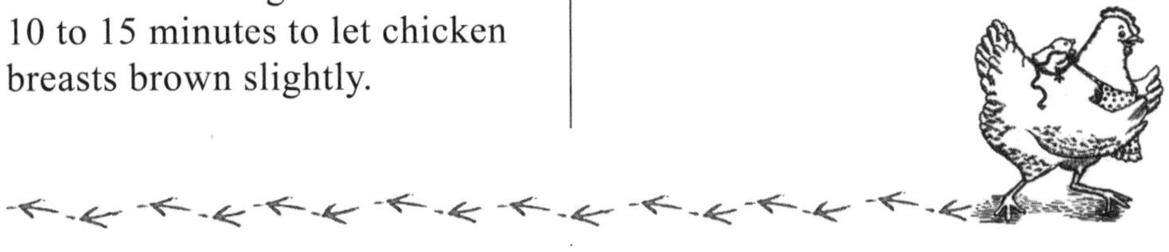

Nacho Chicken

1 chicken, quartered
200 g (7 ounces) processed cheese spread
100 g (3½ ounces) hot salsa
¾ cup (185 ml) milk
3 tablespoons (45 ml) Worcestershire sauce

- Preheat oven to 175° C (350° F).
- Place chicken quarters in sprayed 23 x 33-cm (9 x 13-inch) baking dish with sides.
- Combine cheese spread, salsa, milk and Worcestershire sauce in saucepan and heat just enough to mix well. Spread over chicken.
- Cover and bake for 1 hour. Serves 8 to 10.

One-Dish Chicken Bake

1 30-g (1-ounce) packet vegetable soup mix
170 g (6 ounces) chicken stuffing mix
4 boneless, skinless chicken breast halves
1 280-g (10-ounce) can cream of mushroom soup
⅓ cup (80 g) sour cream

- Preheat oven to 190° C (375° F).
- Toss contents of vegetable soup mix, stuffing mix and 1⅔ cups (400 ml) water in bowl and set aside.
- Place chicken in sprayed 23 x 33-cm (9 x 13-inch) baking dish.
- Mix soup and sour cream in saucepan over low heat just enough to pour over chicken. Spoon stuffing evenly over top.
- Bake for 40 minutes. Serves 4.

Onion-Sweet Chicken

2 chickens, quartered
455 g (16 ounces) whole-berry cranberry sauce
250 ml (8 ounces) Thousand Island salad dressing
1 30-g (1-ounce) packet onion soup mix

- Preheat oven to 175° C (350° F).
- Place chicken quarters in sprayed 25 x 38-cm (10 x 15-inch) baking dish. Combine cranberry sauce, salad dressing and soup mix in bowl, blend well and pour over chicken.
- Cover and bake for 1 hour 10 minutes. Before last 10 minutes, uncover chicken and place back in oven to brown. Serves 6 to 8.

Oven-Glazed Chicken

4 boneless, skinless chicken breast halves
1 280-g (10-ounce) can Italian tomato soup
2 tablespoons (30 ml) Worcestershire sauce
2 tablespoons (30 g) packed brown sugar

- Preheat oven to 175° C (350° F).
- Place chicken breasts in sprayed 18 x 28-cm (7 x 11-inch) baking dish.
- Combine tomato soup, Worcestershire sauce and brown sugar in small bowl and mix well. Spoon over chicken.
- Bake for 1 hour. Serves 4.

Oven-Fried Ranch Chicken

1 medium chicken, cut into serving pieces
1 cup (250 ml) ranch dressing
½ cup (110 g) mayonnaise
2–3 cups (55–85 g) crushed cornflakes

- Preheat oven to 175° C (350° F).
- Pat chicken pieces dry and place on paper towels.
- Combine ranch dressing and mayonnaise in shallow bowl and mix well.
- Dip chicken pieces in dressing and cover well. Roll each piece in cornflakes and coat all sides well.
- Arrange pieces so they do not touch in sprayed 23 x 33-cm (9 x 13-inch) baking dish. Bake for 1 hour. Serves 8.

Q: Why did the chicken cross the road halfway?

A: She wanted to lay it on the line.

Oven-Herb Chicken

½ cup (50 g) grated parmesan cheese
1 tablespoon (2 g) rosemary
1 tablespoon (2 g) thyme leaves
1 teaspoon oregano
1 tablespoon (2 g) parsley flakes
½ teaspoon garlic powder
5–6 boneless, skinless chicken breast halves or 1 chicken, quartered

- Preheat oven to 160° C (325° F).
- Combine parmesan cheese, rosemary, thyme, oregano, parsley, garlic powder, ½ teaspoon salt and 1 teaspoon pepper in medium bowl.
- Dip chicken breasts in herb mixture; coat well.
- Place chicken in sprayed 23 x 33-cm (9 x 13-inch) shallow baking dish. (Do not crowd pieces.) Bake for 1 hour. Serves 8.

Oven-Fried Chicken

⅔ cup (40 g) fine dry breadcrumbs
⅓ cup (35 g) grated parmesan cheese
½ teaspoon garlic salt
½ cup (125 ml) Italian salad dressing
6 boneless, skinless chicken breast halves

- Preheat oven to 175° C (350° F).
- Combine breadcrumbs, cheese and garlic salt in shallow bowl.
- In separate shallow bowl, place salad dressing. Dip chicken in salad dressing and dredge in crumb mixture.
- Place chicken in 23 x 33-cm (9 x 13-inch) sprayed baking pan.
- Bake for 50 minutes. Serves 6.

Oven-Fried Turkey

450–680 g (1–1½ pounds) turkey tenderloins
155 g (5½ ounces) chicken coating mix

- Preheat oven to 205° C (400° F).
- Place all tenderloin strips on several pieces of paper towel to partially dry.
- Pour chicken coating mix into shallow bowl and press both sides of each piece of turkey into seasoned coating.
- Place in sprayed 23 x 33-cm (9 x 13-inch) baking pan so pieces do not touch. Bake for 20 to 30 minutes or until turkey is light brown. Serves 12.

Parmesan-Crusted Chicken

1 egg white, beaten
1½ cups (180 g) dry breadcrumbs
1 teaspoon dried parsley
½ cup (50 g) grated parmesan cheese
4 small boneless, skinless chicken breast halves
Olive oil
¼ cup (25 g) minced shallots
Olive oil
½ cup (125 ml) dry white wine
½ cup (125 ml) whipping cream
½ cup (125 ml) chicken stock
¼ cup (60 g) butter, cubed
¾ teaspoon dried sage

- Preheat oven to 220° C (425° F).
- Combine beaten egg white and 1 tablespoon (15 ml) water in bowl.
- In separate bowl, combine breadcrumbs, parsley, cheese and a little salt and pepper.
- Dip each piece of chicken in egg white and dredge in crumb mixture. Place in heavy frypan with a little oil and sauté chicken until golden on both sides, about 5 minutes.
- Transfer to sprayed 18 x 28-cm (7 x 11-inch) baking dish and bake for 15 minutes.
- Sauté shallots in a little oil in saucepan.
- Add wine, cream and chicken stock. Simmer until it reduces by half. Stir in butter and sage. Serve over parmesan chicken. Serves 4.

Party Chicken Breasts

6 boneless, skinless chicken breast halves
6 strips bacon
1 280-g (10-ounce) can cream of chicken soup
230 g (8 ounces) sour cream

- Preheat oven to 160° C (325° F).
- Wrap each chicken breast with 1 strip bacon and secure with toothpicks.
- Place chicken in sprayed 23 x 33-cm (9 x 13-inch) baking pan.
- Heat soup and sour cream in saucepan, just enough to pour over chicken.
- Bake for 1 hour. Serves 6 to 8.

Peachy Chicken

½ cup (125 ml) Italian dressing
2 teaspoons ground ginger
4 boneless, skinless chicken breast halves
⅓ cup (110 g) peach jam

- Combine Italian dressing and ginger in large resealable plastic bag. Place chicken in plastic bag and turn several times to coat chicken.
- Marinate in refrigerator, turning occasionally, for 4 hours or overnight. When ready to cook, remove chicken and discard marinade. Save ⅓ cup (75 ml) marinade.
- Bring saved marinade in small saucepan to a boil for 1 minute. Remove from heat, stir in peach jam and set aside.
- Grill or bake chicken until juices run clear and brush with mixture in the last 5 minutes of cooking. Serves 4.

Picante Chicken

4 boneless, skinless chicken breast halves
455 g (16 ounces) salsa
4 tablespoons (55 g) brown sugar
1 tablespoon (15 g) mustard
Rice, cooked

- Preheat oven to 190° C (375° F).
- Place chicken in shallow sprayed baking dish.
- Combine salsa, brown sugar and mustard in small bowl and pour over chicken.
- Bake for 45 minutes or until chicken juices run clear and serve over rice. Serves 4.

Rosemary Chicken

½ cup (60 g) flour
1 tablespoon (2 g) dried rosemary
½ cup (125 ml) Italian salad dressing
4–5 boneless, skinless chicken breast halves

- Preheat oven to 175° C (350° F).
- Combine flour and half rosemary in bowl.
- Pour a little Italian dressing in shallow bowl and dip chicken breasts in dressing.
- Dredge chicken in flour mixture. Place in sprayed 23 x 33-cm (9 x 13-inch) baking dish.
- Bake for 40 minutes. Remove from oven and sprinkle remaining rosemary over breasts and cook for an additional 10 minutes. Serves 4.

Capsicum Cheese-Stuffed Fried Chicken

4 boneless, skinless chicken breast halves
½ cup (125 ml) milk
1 large egg, beaten
2 cups (240 g) seasoned breadcrumbs
Olive oil
455 g (16 ounces) processed cheese spread
1 115-g (4-ounce) jar roasted red capsicum, finely chopped

- Preheat oven to 175° C (350° F).
- Dry chicken breasts with paper towels and sprinkle well with a little salt and pepper.
- Combine milk and beaten egg in shallow bowl and mix well. In separate shallow bowl, place breadcrumbs.
- Dip chicken in milk mixture and dredge in breadcrumbs.
- Pour oil to 3 mm (⅛ inch) depth and cook chicken in large frypan over medium-high heat for about 10 to 12 minutes on each side. Transfer to sprayed 23 x 33-cm (9 x 13-inch) baking tray.
- In a bowl, mix roasted capsicum and cheese spread.
- Hold chicken with tongs and cut slit in 1 side of each chicken breast to form pocket. Spoon about ¼ cup (55 g) capsicum cheese mixture into each pocket and bake for about 3 minutes or until cheese melts. Serves 4.

Capsicum-Chicken Enchilada Bake

10 corn tortillas
1 280-g (10-ounce) can cream of mushroom soup
1 280-g (10-ounce) can cream of chicken soup
1 cup (250 ml) milk
1 small onion, chopped
230 g (8 ounces) diced green chillies
2 115-g (4-ounce) jars diced roasted red capsicum, drained
5 boneless, skinless chicken breast halves, cooked
340 g (12 ounces) shredded cheddar cheese

- Preheat oven to 175° C (350° F).
- Cut tortillas into 2-cm (1-inch) strips and lay half of them in sprayed baking dish. Mix mushroom soup, chicken soup, milk, onion, green chillies and roasted red capsicum in saucepan and heat just enough to mix.
- Chop cooked chicken and place half on top of tortilla strips. Pour half of sauce on top of chicken, repeat tortilla layer and sauce layer. Cover and bake for 45 minutes. Sprinkle cheese over casserole, return to oven and bake for an additional 5 minutes. Serves 5.

TIP: If you want to make this dish in advance, top with cheese and refrigerate overnight. Bake the next day when you need it.

Pop's Pleasing Pasta

1 400-g (14-ounce) packet frozen, cooked, breadcrumbed chicken cutlets, thawed
1 800-g (28-ounce) jar spaghetti sauce
280 g (10 ounces) grated parmesan cheese
230 g (8 ounces) thin spaghetti, cooked

- Preheat oven to 205° C (400° F).
- Place cutlets in sprayed 23 x 33-cm (9 x 13-inch) baking dish and top each with about ¼ cup (65 g) spaghetti sauce and a heaped tablespoon (15 ml) parmesan. Bake for 15 minutes.
- Place cooked pasta on serving platter and top with cutlets.
- Sprinkle remaining cheese over cutlets. Heat remaining spaghetti sauce and serve with chicken and spaghetti. Serves 6.

The longest recorded flight of a chicken is 13 seconds.

Spring Chicken

900 g (2 pounds) chicken thighs
Olive oil
¾ cup (205 g) chilli sauce
¾ cup (165 g) packed brown sugar
1 30-g (1-ounce) packet onion soup mix
⅛ teaspoon cayenne pepper
Rice, cooked

- Preheat oven to 160° C (325° F).
- Brown chicken in frypan with oil and place in sprayed 23 x 33-cm (9 x 13-inch) baking dish.
- Combine chilli sauce, brown sugar, dry soup mix, cayenne pepper and ½ cup (125 ml) water in bowl and pour over chicken.
- Cover and bake for 20 minutes. Uncover and bake for an additional 15 minutes. Serve over rice. Serves 8.

Barbecue Ranch Chicken

½ cup (50 g) parmesan cheese
1½ cups (40 g) cornflakes
10 g (½ ounce) barbecue seasoning
900 g (2 pounds) chicken drumsticks
½ cup (115 g) butter, melted

- Preheat oven to 175° C (350° F).
- Combine cheese, cornflakes and barbecue seasoning in bowl.
- Dip washed, dried chicken in melted butter and dredge in cornflake mixture.
- Bake for 50 minutes or until golden brown. Serves 8.

Reuben Chicken

4 boneless, skinless chicken breast halves
4 slices Swiss cheese
1 425-g (15-ounce) can sauerkraut, drained
1 250-ml (8-ounce) bottle Thousand Island salad dressing

- Preheat oven to 175° C (350° F).
- Arrange chicken in sprayed 18 x 28-cm (7 x 11-inch) baking dish.
- Place cheese over chicken and spread sauerkraut next. Cover with dressing.
- Bake, covered, for 30 minutes. Uncover and cook for an additional 15 minutes. Serves 4.

Ritzy Chicken

6 boneless, skinless chicken breast halves
230 g (8 ounces) sour cream
115 g (4 ounces) round buttery crackers, crushed

- Preheat oven to 175° C (350° F).
- Dip chicken in sour cream and roll in cracker crumbs with ¼ teaspoon pepper. Place chicken in sprayed 23 x 33-cm (9 x 13-inch) baking dish.
- Bake for 55 minutes. Serves 6.

Roasted Chicken

1 1.4–1.8-kg (3–4-pound) chicken
3 tablespoons (45 g) butter, softened

- Preheat oven to 175° C (350° F).
- Wash and dry chicken with paper towels. Remove giblet package from cavity. Spread butter over breasts, legs and wings. Salt and pepper liberally.
- Place chicken on back in deep roasting pan. Bake for 1 hour per kilogram or until juices run clear.
- Baste frequently, add water if necessary. Turn bird occasionally to brown evenly. Serves 8.

TIP: Basting with pan juices will make a glazed coating on chicken. For a crusted topping, sprinkle flour over chicken after spreading butter on outside.

Roasted Chicken Supreme

This is such an easy recipe and good for any meal.

1.4-kg (3-pound) whole chicken
1 stick celery
1 onion
Canola oil
Paprika

- Preheat oven to 160° C (325° F).
- Wash chicken and dry with paper towels. Cut celery in half. Insert celery and onion into chicken cavity. Tie legs together, rub chicken with oil and sprinkle with paprika.
- Roast in open pan for 1 hour per kilogram of chicken or until juices run clear. Baste every 40 minutes. To serve, remove onion and celery. (You can save and reuse for soup or stew.) Chicken will be extra juicy and moist with no onion flavour. Serves 6.

Roasted Chicken and Vegetables

2 pounds (900 g) boneless chicken breasts
1 cup (250 ml) lemon pepper marinade with lemon juice, divided
455 g (16 ounces) frozen mixed vegetables, thawed
¼ cup (60 ml) olive oil

- Preheat oven to 190° C (375° F).
- Arrange chicken skin-side down in sprayed 23 x 33-cm (9 x 13-inch) baking dish. Pour ⅔ cup (150 ml) marinade over chicken. Bake for 30 minutes.
- Turn chicken over and baste with remaining ⅓ cup (75 ml) marinade.
- Toss vegetables with olive oil and 1 tablespoon (15 g) salt. Arrange vegetables around chicken and cover with foil. Return dish to oven and bake for an additional 20 to 30 minutes or until juices run clear.

Serves 8 to 10.

In Georgia, America – the chicken capital of the world – it's illegal to eat chicken with a fork.

Pineapple-Teriyaki Chicken

6 boneless, skinless chicken breast halves
½ red onion, sliced
1 green capsicum, seeded, sliced
1 cup (250 ml) teriyaki marinade
425 g (15 ounces) tinned pineapple rings with juice

- Preheat oven to 175° C (350° F).
- Place chicken in sprayed 23 x 33-cm (9 x 13-inch) baking dish and arrange vegetables over chicken.
- Mix teriyaki marinade with juice from pineapple. Pour over vegetables and chicken.
- Bake for 45 minutes. Spoon juices over chicken once during baking.
- About 10 minutes before chicken is done, place pineapple slices over chicken and return to oven. Serves 6.

Saucy Chicken

5–6 boneless, skinless chicken breast halves
450 (16 ounces) thick-and-chunky salsa
1 cup (220 g) packed light brown sugar
1½ tablespoons (25 g) Dijon-style mustard
Rice, cooked

- Preheat oven to 175° C (350° F).
- Place chicken breasts in sprayed 23 x 33-cm (9 x 13-inch) baking dish.
- Combine salsa, sugar and mustard in bowl and pour over chicken.
- Cover and bake for 45 minutes. Serve over rice. Serves 6.

Sunday Chicken

5–6 boneless, skinless chicken breast halves
½ cup (120 g) sour cream
¼ cup (60 ml) soy sauce
1 280-g (10-ounce) can French onion soup

- Preheat oven to 175° C (350° F).
- Place chicken in sprayed 23 x 33-cm (9 x 13-inch) baking dish.
- Combine sour cream, soy sauce and soup in saucepan and heat just enough to mix well. Pour over chicken breasts.
- Cover and bake for 55 minutes. Serves 6.

Saucy Chicken Breasts

This sauce really makes a delicious chicken dish!

1½ cups (335 g) mayonnaise
½ cup (125 ml) cider vinegar
¼ cup (60 ml) lemon juice
⅓ cup (70 g) sugar
3 tablespoons (45 ml) Worcestershire sauce
5 boneless, skinless chicken breast halves

- Combine mayonnaise, vinegar, lemon juice, sugar and Worcestershire sauce in saucepan and mix well with whisk until mixture is smooth.
- Pour half mixture into resealable plastic bag with chicken breasts and marinate for 4 to 6 hours. Move chicken around a couple of times to make sure marinade covers chicken.
- When ready to cook, preheat oven to 175° C (350° F). Place chicken breasts in sprayed 23 x 33-cm (9 x 13-inch) baking dish, arranged so pieces are not touching. Pour remaining half of marinade from bag over chicken. Sprinkle pepper generously over meat.
- Cook for 50 to 60 minutes or until juices run clear. If chicken breasts are not slightly brown, place under griller for 3 to 4 minutes, but watch closely. Serves 6.

Savoury Oven-Fried Chicken

2 cups (55 g) crushed cornflakes
½ cup (50 g) grated parmesan cheese
1 tablespoon (2 g) finely chopped rosemary
1 tablespoon (2 g) thyme leaves
1 teaspoon oregano
1 tablespoon (2 g) finely chopped parsley
1 tablespoon (2 g) crushed garlic
1 tablespoon (2 g) finely chopped basil leaves
½ cup (115 g) butter, melted
8 boneless, skinless chicken breast halves

- Preheat oven to 160° C (325° F).
- Mix cornflakes, parmesan cheese, rosemary, thyme, basil, oregano, parsley, crushed garlic, ½ teaspoon salt and 1 teaspoon pepper in medium bowl.
- In separate bowl, place melted butter. Dip chicken in butter and then cornflake mixture.
- Place in sprayed 23 x 33-cm (9 x 13-inch) baking dish. Do not let pieces touch. Bake for 1 hour. Serves 8.

Springy Chicken

4–5 boneless, skinless chicken breast halves
1 tablespoon (2 g) oregano
¾ teaspoon garlic powder
½ cup (115 g) butter, melted

- Place chicken in resealable plastic bag and add oregano and garlic powder. Marinate in refrigerator for 3 or 4 hours.
- When ready to bake, preheat oven to 160° C (325° F).
- Place chicken and butter in sprayed 23 x 33-cm (9 x 13-inch) baking dish. Cover and bake for 1 hour. Serves 5.

Super-Simple Quails

4 quails
Canola oil
2 teaspoons paprika
Freshly cracked black pepper

- Preheat oven to 175°C (350° F).
- Wash and dry quails and place in sprayed baking pan. Rub outside with oil. Sprinkle paprika, lots of black pepper and a little salt over each.
- Bake for 30 minutes or until juices run clear. Serves 4.

Sesame Chicken

½ cup (60 g) flour
½ teaspoon chilli powder
¼ teaspoon paprika
½ teaspoon onion salt
½ teaspoon celery salt
1 teaspoon lemon pepper
1 teaspoon garlic powder
8 boneless, skinless chicken breast halves
½ cup (115 g) butter, melted
1 cup (130 g) sesame seeds, lightly toasted

- Preheat oven to 175° C (350° F).
- Thoroughly mix flour, chilli powder, paprika, onion salt, celery salt, lemon pepper and garlic powder in bowl.
- Roll chicken breasts in flour mixture and continue to roll chicken until all flour mixture is used.
- Dip floured chicken in butter and roll in sesame seeds. Place chicken breasts in sprayed 25 x 38-cm (10 x 15-inch) baking dish. Pour any extra butter into baking dish and bake for 1 hour. Serves 8.

Q: What is a haunted chicken?

A: A poultry-geist.

Soft Chicken-Taco Bake

6 boneless, skinless chicken breast halves
30 g (1 ounce) taco seasoning
1 425-g (15-ounce) can kidney beans, rinsed and drained
1 large onion, chopped
12 corn tortillas
1 cup (250 ml) unthickened cream
3 large tomatoes, chopped
1 tablespoon (2 g) minced coriander
340 g (12 ounces) shredded cheddar cheese
1 145-g (5-ounce) package instant Spanish rice

- Preheat oven to 160° C (325° F).
- Boil chicken in just enough water to cover. When chicken cooks and is tender, season with taco seasoning and 1 tablespoon (10 g) salt. Cool and chop or shred chicken.
- Place several tablespoons meat, several tablespoons beans and 1 teaspoon onion in middle of each tortilla. Roll and place side by side in sprayed 23 x 33-cm (9 x 13-inch) baking dish. Pour cream over rolled tortillas.
- Combine tomatoes, remaining onion and coriander and sprinkle evenly over rolled tortillas. Spread cheese over top of tomatoes and bake for 20 minutes or until cheese melts. Serve hot with Spanish rice. Serves 6.

Chicken-on-the-Border

8 boneless, skinless chicken breast halves
1 cup (115 g) shredded mozzarella cheese
½ cup (60 g) shredded cheddar cheese
115 g (4 ounces) chopped green chillies
1 teaspoon coriander
3 tablespoons (30 g) onion flakes
⅓ cup (75 g) butter
2 teaspoons ground cumin
1 teaspoon chilli powder
1 cup (55 g) crushed corn chips

- Preheat oven to 175° C (350° F).
- Pound chicken breasts to about 5 mm (¼ inch) thick. Mix cheeses, chillies, coriander and onion in bowl.
- Place 2 to 3 tablespoons (15 to 20 g) cheese mixture on each chicken breast and roll and place seam-side down in sprayed 23 x 33-cm (9 x 13-inch) baking dish. Melt butter in saucepan, add cumin and chilli powder and pour over chicken.
- Cover and bake for 30 minutes, uncover and top with crushed chips. Return to oven and bake for an additional 15 minutes. Serves 8.

Southern-Stuffed Capsicums

6 large green capsicums
230 g (½ pound) chicken livers, chopped
6 slices bacon, diced
1 cup (160 g) chopped onion
1 cup (100 g) sliced celery
1 clove garlic, crushed
1 115-g (4-ounce) can sliced mushrooms
2 cups (330 g) cooked rice

- Preheat oven to 190° C (375° F).
- Wash capsicums, cut slice through stem end and remove seeds. Cook for about 5 minutes in small amount of boiling, salted water. Remove from water and drain.
- Cook chicken livers, bacon, onion, celery, garlic and 1 teaspoon salt in medium saucepan until vegetables are tender. Add mushrooms and rice; mix well. Stuff capsicums with mixture.
- Arrange in sprayed baking pan, add 1 cm (½ inch) water, cover and bake for 20 to 25 minutes. This dish can also be frozen before cooking if you want to prepare it ahead of time. Simply thaw before placing the dish in the oven. Serves 6.

Spiced Mexican Chicken

2 cups (190 g) instant rice
4 boneless, skinless, cooked chicken breast halves, cut into strips
1 425-g (15-ounce) can Mexican stewed tomatoes with liquid
230 g (8 ounces) tomato simmer sauce
425 g (15 ounces) tinned corn kernels, drained
1 115-g (4-ounce) jar diced roasted red capsicum, drained
1 teaspoon chilli powder
1 teaspoon ground cumin

- Preheat oven to 175° C (350° F).
- Spread rice evenly in sprayed 3-L (3-quart) baking dish. Place chicken strips over top of rice.
- Combine Mexican tomatoes, simmer sauce, corn, roasted red capsicum, chilli powder, cumin and ½ teaspoon each of salt and pepper in large bowl and mix well.
- Slowly and gently pour mixture over chicken and rice. Cover and bake for 1 hour. Serves 6.

Southwest-Mexican Pizzas

Butter
6 20-cm (8-inch) flour tortillas
1 400-g (14-ounce) jar chilli con carne simmer sauce
1½ cups (210 g) cooked, shredded chicken
1 jalapeno chilli, roasted, peeled and chopped
4 spring onions, finely diced
230 g (8 ounces) shredded cheddar cheese

- Preheat oven to 220° C (425° F).
- Butter 1 side of each tortilla and place tortillas, butter-side up, on baking trays. Bake for 4 to 5 minutes, just enough to crisp tortillas.
- Spread each tortilla with about ¼ to ⅓ cup (70 to 90 g) sauce, shredded chicken, chilli and spring onions. Top with shredded cheese.
- Return to oven and bake just until cheese melts. Cut into wedges to serve. Serves 6.

TIP: If you don't want to add the jalapeno chilli, just use a red capsicum.

Spicy Chicken and Rice

3 cups (420 g) cooked, sliced chicken
2 cups (390 g) cooked brown rice
200 g (7 ounces) processed cheese spread
100 g (3½ ounces) hot salsa
1 280-g (10-ounce) can chopped tomatoes
50 g (1½ ounces) sliced green chillies

- Preheat oven to 175° C (350° F).
- Combine chicken, rice, cheese, salsa, tomatoes and green chillies in bowl and mix well.
- Spoon mixture into sprayed 3-L (3-quart) baking dish.
- Cover and bake for 45 minutes. Serves 5.

Sunshine Chicken

1 chicken, quartered
Flour
1 cup (270 g) barbecue sauce
½ cup (125 ml) orange juice

- Preheat oven to 175° C (350° F).
- Place chicken in bowl of flour and coat well.
- Brown chicken in frypan and place in sprayed 23 x 33-cm (9 x 13-inch) baking dish.
- Combine barbecue sauce and orange juice in bowl. Pour over chicken.
- Cover and bake for 45 minutes. Remove from oven, spoon sauce over chicken and bake uncovered for an additional 20 minutes. Serves 4.

Succulent Pecan Chicken Breasts

⅓ cup (75 g) butter
1 cup (120 g) flour
1 cup (110 g) finely ground pecans
¼ cup (30 g) sesame seeds
1 tablespoon (15 g) paprika
1 egg, beaten
1 cup (250 ml) buttermilk*
6 boneless, skinless chicken breast halves
⅓ cup (40 g) coarsely chopped pecans
Fresh parsley

- Preheat oven to 175° C (350° F).
- Melt butter in large 23 x 33-cm (9 x 13-inch) baking dish and set aside. Combine flour, finely ground pecans, sesame seeds, paprika, 1 teaspoon salt and ¼ teaspoon pepper in bowl.
- In separate bowl, combine egg and buttermilk. Dip chicken in egg mixture, dredge in flour mixture and coat well.
- Place chicken in baking dish and turn once to coat with butter. Sprinkle with chopped pecans and bake for 40 minutes or until golden brown. Garnish with fresh parsley. Serves 6 to 8.

TIP: Chicken may be cut into strips, prepared the same way and used as a starter. A honey-mustard dressing would be nice for dipping. This recipe could also be used for fish, like orange roughy, if cooking time is reduced to half.

**TIP: To make buttermilk, mix 1 cup (250 ml) milk with 1 tablespoon (15 ml) lemon juice or vinegar and let milk rest for about 10 minutes.*

Sweet-and-Sour Chicken

6 boneless, skinless chicken breast halves
Olive oil
1 30-g (1-ounce) packet onion soup mix
170 ml (6 ounces) orange juice

- Preheat oven to 175° C (350° F).
- Brown chicken in a little oil or butter and place chicken in sprayed 23 x 33-cm (9 x 13-inch) baking dish.
- Combine onion soup mix, orange juice and ⅔ cup (150 ml) water in small bowl. Mix well and pour over chicken.
- Bake for 45 to 50 minutes. Serves 6.

Super Cheese Chicken

1 280-g (10-ounce) can cream of chicken soup
1 cup (185 g) brown rice
4–6 boneless, skinless chicken breast halves
230 g (8 ounces) shredded cheddar cheese

- Preheat oven to 175° C (350° F).
- Combine soup, rice, 1½ cups (375 ml) water and a little salt and pepper in bowl.
- Place in 23 x 33-cm (9 x 13-inch) baking dish.
- Sprinkle chicken with additional pepper and place in baking dish with rice-soup mixture.
- Cover and bake for 50 minutes. Uncover, sprinkle cheese over chicken and serve. Serves 6.

Tangy Chicken

900 g (2 pounds) chicken pieces
3 tablespoons (45 g) butter
½ cup (135 g) steak sauce

- Preheat oven to 175° C (350° F).
- Brown chicken in frypan with butter and place in sprayed 23 x 33-cm (9 x 13-inch) baking dish.
- Combine sauce and ½ cup (125 ml) water and pour over chicken.
- Cover and bake for 45 minutes. Uncover last 10 minutes of cooking time for chicken to brown. Chicken is done when juices run clear. Serves 6.

Tasty Turkey Crunch

1 230-g (8-ounce) package noodles
2½ cups (350 g) cooked, diced turkey
280 g (10 ounces) chicken gravy
2 cups (120 g) round, buttery cracker crumbs

- Preheat oven to 175° C (350° F).
- Boil noodles according to package directions and drain.
- Arrange alternating layers of noodles, turkey and gravy in sprayed 2-L (2-quart) baking dish and cover with cracker crumbs.
- Bake for 35 minutes. Serves 6.

Turkey Burgers

900 g (2 pounds) minced turkey
455 g (16 ounces) hot barbecue salsa
8 slices cheddar cheese
Sesame seed hamburger buns

- Combine turkey with 1 cup (265 g) salsa in large bowl. Mix well and shape into 8 patties.
- Place patties in frypan and fry for 12 to 15 minutes. Turn once during cooking. Top each patty with a cheese slice and grill just long enough to melt cheese.
- Place burgers on buns, spoon a heaped tablespoon (15 ml) salsa over cheese and top with remaining half of bun. Serves 8.

Winey Chicken

6 boneless, skinless chicken breast halves
Olive oil
1 280-g (10-ounce) can cream of mushroom soup
1 280-g (10-ounce) can French onion soup
1 cup (250 ml) white wine
Rice, cooked

- Preheat oven to 160° C (325° F).
- Brown chicken in frypan with a little bit of oil. Place in 23 x 33-cm (9 x 13-inch) baking dish.
- Combine soups and wine and pour over chicken.
- Cover and bake for 35 minutes. Uncover and bake for an additional 25 minutes. Serve over rice. Serves 6 to 8.

Birds of a Feather: Frys, Grills and Sautés

Make your brood happy in a snap with these quick and easy chicken sautés and frys. Grilling doesn't get any easier!

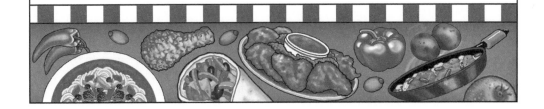

Birds of a Feather: Frys, Grills and Sautés Contents

Birds of a Feather: Frys, Grills and Sautés Contents

American Chicken

2 cups (280 g) cooked chicken breast halves, sliced into strips
1 cup (100 g) sliced celery
1½ cups (250 g) cooked rice
1 tablespoon (15 g) butter
2 tablespoons (15 g) flour
1½ cups (375 ml) chicken stock

- Combine chicken and celery in bowl and mix with rice, 1 teaspoon salt and ⅛ teaspoon pepper. Melt butter in frypan and make into smooth paste with flour.
- Add stock slowly and stir constantly. Bring to a boil and continue stirring.
- Add chicken and rice mixture and heat thoroughly. Serves 6.

Asparagus Chicken

2 large boneless, skinless chicken breasts, cut into strips
Olive oil
1 tablespoon (15 ml) lemon juice
250 ml (8 ounces) hollandaise sauce
230 g (8 ounces) egg noodles, cooked
1 425-g (15-ounce) can asparagus spears

- Cook chicken strips in large frypan with a little oil for 12 to 15 minutes or until brown and stir occasionally.
- Add hollandaise sauce and lemon juice. Cover and cook for an additional 10 minutes, stirring occasionally.
- When ready to serve, place chicken over noodles and add hot asparagus spears. Serves 6.

Asparagus and Cheese Chicken

1 tablespoon (15 g) butter
4 boneless, skinless chicken breast halves
1 280-g (10-ounce) can cream of asparagus soup
280 g (10 ounces) asparagus, chopped
⅓ cup (85 ml) milk
80 g (3 ounces) processed cheese spread

- Heat butter in frypan and cook chicken for 10 to 15 minutes or until brown on both sides. Remove chicken and set aside.
- In same frypan, combine soup, asparagus and milk. Heat to boiling. Return chicken to frypan and reduce heat to low.
- Cover and cook for an additional 25 minutes until chicken is no longer pink and asparagus is tender. Serves 4.

Cheesy Chicken and Potatoes

560 g (20 ounces) frozen hash browns, thawed and shredded
100 g (3½ ounces) red capsicum, diced
Olive oil
1 tablespoon (15 g) minced garlic
2–2½ cups (280–600 g) bite-size chunks roast chicken
1 bunch springs onions, sliced
1 cup (115 g) shredded cheddar cheese

- Cook hash browns and capsicum in a little oil in large frypan over medium-high heat for 7 minutes and turn frequently.
- Add garlic, chicken, spring onions and ⅓ cup (75 ml) water and cook for 5 to 6 minutes. Remove from heat and stir in cheese. Serve immediately. Serves 8.

Chicken and Sauerkraut

6 large, boneless, skinless chicken breast halves
1 425 g (15-ounce) can sliced potatoes, drained
1 455 g (16-ounce) can sauerkraut, drained
¼ cup (30 g) pine nuts

- Season chicken with a little black pepper and cook in large frypan over medium heat for 15 minutes or until chicken browns on both sides.
- Add potatoes to frypan and spoon sauerkraut over potatoes. Cover and cook over low heat for 35 minutes or until chicken is done.
- Toast pine nuts in dry frypan on medium heat until golden brown. Stir constantly. Sprinkle chicken and sauerkraut with toasted pine nuts and serve. Serves 6.

TIP: This is good served with sour cream.

Chicken and Prawn Curry

2 280-g (10-ounce) cans cream of chicken soup
⅓ cup (85 ml) milk
1½ teaspoons curry powder
340 g (12 ounces) cooked, chopped chicken
170 g (6 ounces) frozen prawns, peeled and veined
Rice, cooked

- Heat soup, milk and curry powder in saucepan. Stir in chicken pieces and prawns.
- Serve over buttered rice. Serves 6.

Chicken and Wild Rice Special

170 g (6 ounces) mixed long grain and wild rice
4–5 boneless, skinless chicken breast halves
Olive oil
2 280-g (10-ounce) cans French onion soup
1 red capsicum, julienned
1 green capsicum, julienned

- Cook rice in saucepan and keep warm. Brown chicken breasts on both sides in large frypan with a little oil over medium-high heat.
- Add soup, ¾ cup (175 ml) water and capsicums. Reduce heat to medium-low, cover and cook for 15 minutes.
- To serve, place rice on serving platter with chicken breasts on top. Serve sauce in gravy boat to pour over chicken and rice. Serves 5.

TIP: For a thicker sauce, spoon 2 or 3 tablespoons (30 to 45 ml) sauce into a small bowl and stir in 2 tablespoons (20 g) flour. Mix well and stir in onion soup. Heat and stir constantly until sauce thickens.

Q: What do you call a frightened scuba diver?

A: Chicken of the sea.

Chicken and the Works

6 boneless, skinless chicken breast halves
Olive oil
2 280-g (10-ounce) cans cream of chicken soup
2 cups (190 g) instant white rice
280 g (10 ounces) frozen green peas, thawed

- Sprinkle chicken with black pepper and brown in large frypan with a little oil. Reduce heat, cover and simmer for about 15 minutes. Transfer chicken to plate and keep warm.
- Add soup, 2 cups (500 ml) water and mix well. Heat to boiling and stir in rice and green peas. Top with chicken breasts, cover and simmer over low heat for about 10 minutes. Serves 6.

Chicken Cacciatore

1 1.1-kg (2½-pound) frying chicken
Olive oil
2 onions, sliced
1 425-g (15-ounce) can tomatoes
230 g (8 ounces) tomato simmer sauce
1 teaspoon dried oregano
1 teaspoon celery seed

- Quarter chicken and sprinkle with plenty of salt and black pepper. Place in large frypan on medium-high heat with a little oil. Add sliced onions and cook until chicken is tender, about 15 minutes.
- Add tomatoes, simmer sauce, oregano and celery seed. Bring mixture to a boil, reduce heat and simmer for about 20 minutes. Serves 6.

TIP: This is great over hot cooked noodles or spaghetti.

Chicken Couscous

160 g (5½ ounces) couscous, cooked
1 roast chicken, boned and cubed
1 425-g (15-ounce) can baby green peas, drained
⅓ cup (50 g) sultanas
50 g (2 ounces) pine nuts, toasted and crushed

- Combine couscous, chicken, peas, sultanas and pine nuts in microwave-safe dish. Heat on medium for about 2 minutes or until mixture is warm and stir once. Serves 6.

Chicken Curry

2 280-g (10-ounce) cans cream of mushroom soup
2 teaspoons curry powder
⅓ cup (65 g) chopped almonds, toasted
4 boneless, skinless chicken breast halves, cooked, cubed
White rice, cooked

- Combine soup, 1 soup can water, curry powder, almonds and cubed chicken in large saucepan.
- Heat and stir frequently.
- When ready to serve, spoon over white rice. Serves 4.

Chicken Marseilles

3 tablespoons (45 g) butter
5–6 boneless, skinless chicken breast halves
1 30-g (1-ounce) packet vegetable soup mix
½ teaspoon dill
½ cup (120 g) sour cream
Brown rice, cooked

- Melt butter in frypan, brown chicken for about 10 to 15 minutes and turn occasionally.
- Stir 2 cups (500 ml) water, soup mix and dill into frypan and bring to a boil.
- Reduce heat, cover and simmer, stirring occasionally for 25 to 30 minutes or until chicken is tender.
- Place chicken on a serving dish with hot brown rice. Add sour cream to frypan and stir until creamy.
- Spoon sauce over chicken. Serves 6.

Chicken Elegant

3 tablespoons (45 g) butter
3 tablespoons (20 g) flour
1¾ cups milk
½ cup (60 g) shredded sharp cheddar cheese
½ cup (55 g) shredded Swiss cheese
½ teaspoon Worcestershire sauce
1 cup (140 g) cooked, diced chicken or turkey
1 cup (140 g) cooked, diced ham
1 115-g (4-ounce) can sliced mushrooms, drained
2 tablespoons (30 g) chopped roasted red capsicum
Noodles, cooked

- Melt butter in saucepan and blend in flour. Add milk all at once, then cook and stir until sauce is thick and bubbly. Remove from heat, add cheeses and stir until they melt.
- Stir in Worcestershire sauce, chicken or turkey, ham, mushrooms and capsicum. Heat thoroughly and serve over noodles. Serves 8.

Chicken Fajitas

900 g (2 pounds) boneless, skinless chicken breast halves
1 onion, thinly sliced
1 red capsicum, seeded and sliced
1 teaspoon ground cumin
1½ teaspoons chilli powder
1 tablespoon (15 ml) lime juice
½ cup (125 ml) chicken stock
8–10 warmed flour tortillas
Guacamole
Sour cream
Lettuce and tomatoes

- Cut chicken into diagonal strips and place in large frypan. Add onion, capsicum, cumin, chilli powder, lime juice and chicken stock, cover and cook over medium heat for 25 minutes.
- When serving, spoon chicken mixture with sauce into centre of each warm tortilla and fold.
- Serve with guacamole, sour cream, lettuce or tomatoes or plain. Serves 8.

Simple Chicken in Wine

¼ cup (60 g) butter
4 large boneless, skinless chicken breast halves
1 cup (100 g) diced celery
½ cup (115 g) seeded, diced green or red capsicum
½ cup (80 g) minced onion
1½ cups (375 ml) white wine

- Melt butter in large frypan over medium-high heat and brown chicken on all sides. Remove chicken and set aside.
- Sauté celery, capsicum and onion in saucepan until onion is translucent.
- Pour in wine and stir. Return chicken to frypan, cover and cook for about 1 hour or until juices run clear. Baste with pan juices several times while chicken cooks. Serves 4.

Chicken and Broccoli Rice

3 cups (420 g) cooked, cubed chicken
455 g (16 ounces) frozen broccoli florets
230 g (8 ounces) cubed processed cheese
⅔ cup (150 g) mayonnaise
Rice, cooked

- Combine chicken, broccoli, cheese and ¼ cup (60 ml) water in frypan.
- Cover and cook over medium heat until broccoli is tender but crisp and cheese melts.
- Stir in mayonnaise and heat through, but do not boil. Serve over rice. Serves 6.

Salsa-Grilled Chicken

4–5 boneless, skinless chicken breast halves
1 cup (265 g) thick-and-chunky salsa
¼ cup (55 g) packed dark brown sugar
1 tablespoon (15 g) Dijon-style mustard

- Pound chicken to about 1 cm (½ inch) thick. Combine remaining ingredients in large bowl. Add chicken to bowl, coat with marinade and marinate for 3 to 4 hours in refrigerator.
- Barbecue over hot coals or cook under griller until juices run clear. Serves 4 to 5.

Barbecued Chicken with Raspberry-Barbecue Sauce

340 g (12 ounces) seedless raspberry jam
½ cup (135 g) bottled barbecue sauce
2 tablespoons (30 ml) raspberry vinegar
2 tablespoons (30 g) Dijon-style mustard
1.1-kg (2½-pound) chicken, quartered

- Combine jam, barbecue sauce, vinegar and mustard into a bowl.
- Season chicken quarters liberally with salt and pepper. Barbecue chicken, covered, at medium-high heat for about 8 minutes on each side. Combine all ingredients for Raspberry-Barbecue sauce and baste sauce over quarters during last 2 minutes of cooking.
- Serve with remaining sauce. Serves 8.

Chicken-Risoni Dinner

145 g (5 ounces) risoni
200 g (7 ounces) cooked chicken strips
280 g (10 ounces) frozen corn
280 g (10 ounces) frozen, sliced green beans
¼ cup (60 ml) extra-virgin olive oil
1 teaspoon minced garlic
½ teaspoon chicken stock powder

- Cook risoni according to package directions. Add chicken strips, corn, green beans, olive oil, garlic, chicken stock, ¼ cup (60 ml) water and a little salt and pepper and mix well.
- Cook on low heat and stir several times until mixture is hot, for about 10 to 15 minutes. Serves 4.

Alfredo-Chicken Spaghetti

230 g (8 ounces) thin spaghetti, broken into thirds
2 teaspoons minced garlic
1 455-g (16-ounce) jar alfredo sauce
¼ cup (60 ml) milk
280 g (10 ounces) frozen broccoli florets, thawed
2 cups (280 g) cooked, diced chicken

- Cook pasta according to package directions and drain. Place back in saucepan and stir in garlic, alfredo sauce and milk and mix well.
- Add drained broccoli florets and cook on medium heat for about 5 minutes and stir several times or until broccoli is tender.
- Add more milk if mixture gets too dry. Stir in diced chicken and spoon into serving bowl. Serves 8.

Creamy Chicken and Broccoli

5 large boneless, skinless chicken breast halves, thawed
Olive oil
2 280-g (10-ounce) cans creamy chicken soup
½ cup (125 ml) milk
455 g (16 ounces) frozen broccoli florets, thawed
2 cups (390 g) cooked instant brown rice

- Sprinkle chicken with salt and pepper and brown breasts in oil in large frypan with lid.
- Mix both cans soup and milk in saucepan. Cook over medium heat until soups and milk mix thoroughly. Stir frequently.
- Ladle soup mixture over top of chicken; reduce heat, cover and simmer for 20 minutes.
- Place broccoli around chicken and return heat to high until broccoli is hot. Reduce heat and simmer for about 10 minutes. Serve chicken and sauce over brown rice. Serves 5.

What do you get when you cross a chick with an alley cat?

A peeping tom.

Almond Chicken

4 boneless, skinless chicken breast halves
3 tablespoons (45 g) butter
170 ml (6 ounces) orange juice
2 tablespoons (30 ml) bourbon
Rice, cooked
½ cup (45 g) chopped, salted almonds, toasted

- Brown chicken in butter in frypan over medium heat, then reduce heat to low. Add orange juice, ½ teaspoon salt and ¼ teaspoon pepper.
- Cover and cook over medium heat for 25 minutes. Spoon sauce over chicken twice while it cooks. Remove chicken to serving platter and keep warm.
- Add bourbon to sauce in frypan, stir and heat. Pour mixture over chicken and serve over rice. Sprinkle with almonds.
Serves 4.

Creamy Mushroom Chicken

4 boneless, skinless chicken breast halves
Olive oil
1 280-g (10-ounce) can cream of mushroom soup
1 115-g (4-ounce) can sliced mushrooms, drained
½ cup (125 ml) milk

- Sprinkle chicken liberally with a little salt and pepper. Brown chicken on both sides with a little oil in frypan over high heat.
- While chicken browns, combine mushroom soup, mushrooms and milk in saucepan and heat just enough to mix well.
- Pour over chicken breasts, reduce heat to low and simmer covered for 15 minutes.
Serves 4.

Grilled Chicken with Coleslaw

1 1.6-kg (3½-pound) chicken, quartered
3 tablespoons (45 ml) olive oil
⅔ cup (180 g) barbecue sauce
¼ cup (55 g) mayonnaise
3 tablespoons (45 ml) cider vinegar
2 tablespoons (25 g) sugar
1 340-g (12-ounce) package coleslaw vegetables

- Brush chicken quarters with oil and sprinkle with salt and pepper.
- Grill for 30 to 35 minutes, turning once or twice or until juices run clear when thigh part is pierced and a meat thermometer inserted registers 80° C (175° F).
- Brush with barbecue sauce and grill just until sauce is brown, but not charred.
- Combine mayonnaise, vinegar and sugar in bowl and mix well. Spoon over coleslaw and toss. Refrigerate until ready to serve. Serves 6 to 8.

Crunchy Chip Chicken

1½ cups (85 g) crushed sour cream potato chips
1 tablespoon (2 g) dried parsley
1 egg, beaten
1 tablespoon (15 ml) Worcestershire sauce
4 large boneless, skinless chicken breast halves
¼ cup (60 ml) olive oil

- Combine potato chips and parsley in shallow bowl.
- In separate shallow bowl, combine beaten egg, Worcestershire sauce and 1 tablespoon (15 ml) water.
- Dip chicken pieces in egg mixture, then dredge chicken in potato chip mixture. Heat oil in heavy frypan and fry chicken pieces in oil for about 10 minutes.
- Turn each piece over and cook for an additional 10 minutes until golden brown or until juices run clear. Serves 4.

A chicken can travel at up to 15 kilometres an hour.

Dijon Frypan Chicken

¼ cup (60 ml) ranch salad dressing
1 tablespoon (15 g) Dijon mustard
4 boneless, skinless chicken breast halves
2 tablespoons (30 g) butter
3 tablespoons (45 ml) white wine or chicken stock
Rice, cooked

- Combine salad dressing and mustard in salad bowl and set aside.
- Cook chicken in butter in frypan and simmer for 10 to 15 minutes.
- Add wine or stock and simmer for an additional 20 minutes.
- Whisk in mustard mixture, cook and stir until it blends and is thoroughly hot. Serve over rice. Serves 4.

Deep-Fried Chicken

1 whole chicken, cut up
1 cup (120 g) flour
2 eggs
2 cups (500 ml) milk
1 teaspoon lemon juice

- Wash chicken and pat dry with paper towels. Season chicken with a little salt and pepper. Combine flour, eggs, milk and lemon juice in bowl and mix thoroughly.
- Dredge chicken in batter and fry in deep fryer over medium-high heat until golden brown. Serves 6.

Creamy Tarragon Chicken

1½ cups (180 g) flour
6 boneless, skinless chicken breast halves
2 tablespoons (30 ml) oil
400 ml (14 ounces) chicken stock
1 cup (250 ml) milk
2 teaspoons dried tarragon
1 115-g (4-ounce) can sliced mushrooms, drained
2 230-g (8-ounce) packages chicken flavoured rice

- Mix flour and a little salt and pepper on baking paper and coat chicken. Save extra flour.
- Heat oil in large frypan over medium-high heat and cook chicken breasts, turning once, for about 10 minutes or until light brown. Transfer to plate.
- In same frypan, stir in 2 tablespoons (15 g) flour-salt mixture. Whisk in chicken stock, milk and tarragon, then heat and stir constantly until bubbly. Add mushrooms and return chicken to frypan.
- Cover and simmer for 10 to 15 minutes or until sauce thickens. Cook rice according to package directions and place on serving platter. Spoon chicken and sauce over rice. Serves 6.

Easy Green Chilli Chicken

6 boneless, skinless chicken breast halves
Flour
Olive oil
1 onion, chopped
2 sticks celery, chopped
3 tablespoons (45 ml) white wine vinegar
4 tablespoons (60 ml) Worcestershire sauce
1 cup (250 ml) white wine
1 200-g (7-ounce) jar chopped green chillies
Rice, cooked

- Season chicken with salt and pepper. Dredge chicken in flour, brown in hot oil in frypan and remove from heat.
- Combine onion, celery, vinegar, Worcestershire sauce, wine and green chillies in bowl and mix well. Pour mixture over chicken in frypan, cover and cook for about 30 to 45 minutes.
- Uncover and cook until chicken juices are clear and chicken breasts are slightly brown. Serve over rice. Serves 6 to 8.

According to National Geographic, scientists have settled the old dispute over which came first – the chicken or the egg. They say that reptiles were laying eggs thousands of years before chickens appeared, and the first chicken came from an egg laid by a bird that was not quite a chicken. Clearly, the egg came first.

Fried Chicken Breasts

4 boneless, skinless chicken breast halves
2 eggs, beaten
¾ cup (45 g) cracker crumbs

- Pound chicken breasts to ½ cm (¼ inch) thick.
- Combine eggs, ¼ teaspoon pepper and 2 tablespoons (30 ml) water.
- Dip chicken in egg mixture then in cracker crumbs and coat well. Deep fry until golden brown and drain well. Serves 4.

Fried Chicken Livers

450 g (1 pound) chicken livers, washed, dried
2 tablespoons (30 ml) milk
2 eggs, beaten
Flour
Canola oil

- Season chicken livers with pepper. Add milk to beaten eggs and dip livers into egg mixture. Roll in flour and coat livers well.
- Heat about ½ cm (¼ inch) oil in heavy frypan and brown livers on both sides. Lower heat and cook until tender, about 15 to 20 minutes.
- Remove from frypan, drain on paper towels, salt and pepper again and serve immediately. Serves 4.

Glazed Chicken and Rice

4 boneless, skinless chicken breast halves, cubed
Olive oil
1 570-g (20-ounce) can pineapple chunks with juice
½ cup (135 g) honey-mustard sauce
1 red capsicum, chopped
1 cup (165 g) cooked instant rice

- Brown chicken in frypan with a little oil and cook over low heat for 15 minutes. Add pineapple, honey-mustard sauce and capsicum and bring to a boil.
- Reduce heat to low and simmer for 10 to 15 minutes or until sauce thickens slightly. Serve over rice. Serves 8.

Grilled Chicken Cordon Bleu

6 boneless, skinless chicken breast halves
6 slices Swiss cheese
6 thin slices deli ham
3 tablespoons (45 ml) olive oil
1 cup (120 g) seasoned breadcrumbs

- Flatten chicken breasts to ½ cm (¼ inch) thick and place 1 slice cheese and 1 slice ham on each piece of chicken to within ½ cm (¼ inch) of edges.
- Fold in half and secure with toothpicks. Brush chicken with oil and roll in breadcrumbs.
- Grill, covered, over medium-hot heat for 15 to 18 minutes or until juices run clear. Serves 6.

Barbecued Chicken Fajitas

6 boneless, skinless chicken breast halves
¼ cup (30 g) sesame seeds
⅛ teaspoon cayenne pepper
1 red or green capsicum
1 onion
12 flour tortillas, warmed

- Pound chicken breasts between pieces of baking paper to flatten. Sprinkle both sides of chicken breasts with sesame seeds, cayenne pepper and salt.
- Slice capsicum into strips and slice onion twice to make 3 thick slices.
- Barbecue chicken breasts, capsicum and onion over charcoal fire. Cook for about 5 minutes on each side. Cut chicken breasts into thin strips.
- To assemble, place several strips of chicken, capsicum and onion in centre of tortilla. Fold over and serve. Serves 6.

TIP: Traditional fajitas do not include sour cream, guacamole or chopped avocado, but you don't have to be traditional.

Gourmet Chicken

2 small chickens, skinned and quartered
Flour
Olive oil
1 425-g (15-ounce) can sliced pineapple with juice
1 cup (200 g) sugar
3 tablespoons (25 g) cornflour
¾ cup (175 ml) vinegar
1 tablespoon (15 ml) soy sauce
¼ teaspoon ground ginger
2 chicken stock cubes
1 tablespoon (15 ml) lemon juice
2 green capsicums, cut in strips
White rice, cooked

- Preheat oven to 175° C (350° F).
- Wash chicken and pat dry with paper towel. Coat chicken with salt, pepper and flour. Brown chicken quarters in oil and place in sprayed 25 x 38-cm (10 x 15-inch) roasting pan.
- To make sauce, drain pineapple juice into 2-cup jug. Add water or orange juice to make 1½ cups (375 ml).
- Combine sugar, cornflour, pineapple juice, vinegar, soy sauce, ginger, stock cubes and lemon juice in medium saucepan and bring to a boil.
- Stir constantly for about 2 minutes or until sauce thickens and becomes clear. Pour over browned chicken. Cover and bake for about 40 minutes.
- Place pineapple slices and capsicum on top of chicken and bake for 10 to 15 minutes longer. Serve over rice. Serves 8.

Barbecued Lemon Chicken

2 teaspoons garlic salt
1 tablespoon (20 g) freshly grated lemon peel
2 teaspoons dried thyme leaves
6 boneless, skinless chicken breast halves

- Combine garlic salt, lemon peel, thyme leaves and a little pepper in small bowl. Heat barbecue and spray hotplate.
- Sprinkle seasoning mixture over chicken breasts. Barbecue chicken for 20 to 25 minutes or until chicken is no longer pink and juices run clear. Turn once during cooking. Serves 6.

Italian Chicken and Rice

3 boneless chicken breasts halves, cut into strips
400 g (14 ounces) chicken stock seasoned with Italian herbs
¾ cup (70 g) rice
¼ cup (25 g) grated parmesan cheese

- Cook chicken in non-stick frypan until brown, stirring often, then set aside.
- Add stock and rice to frypan and heat to boil. Cover and simmer over low heat for 25 minutes. (Add water if necessary.)
- Stir in cheese and return chicken to pan. Cover and cook for 5 minutes or until done. Serves 6.

Italian Chicken over Couscous

450 g (1 pound) frozen chicken tenderloins, halved
Olive oil
1 clove garlic, minced
1 onion, chopped
1 425-g (15-ounce) can Italian tomatoes
⅔ cup (85 g) pitted kalamata olives
170 g (6 ounces) couscous

- Season chicken with a little salt and pepper. Place in large frypan with a little oil.
- Add onion and chicken, cover and cook over medium-high heat for about 8 minutes, turning once. Add tomatoes and olives, cover and cook for an additional 8 minutes.
- Prepare couscous according to package directions.
- Spoon couscous onto serving plates and top with chicken and sauce. Serves 8.

Spanish Rice

1 230-g (8-ounce) package Spanish rice mix
170 g (6 ounces) chicken breast strips
1 300-g (11-ounce) can corn
60 g (2 ounces) chopped black olives

- Combine Spanish rice mix and 2¼ cups (560 ml) water in soup pot or large saucepan. Heat to boiling, reduce heat and cook slowly for 5 minutes.
- Add chicken, corn and black olives. Heat to boiling, reduce heat and simmer for about 20 minutes. Serves 4.

TIP: You could also add leftover ham or salami and 1 tablespoon (15 ml) lemon juice to mix it up a little. If you want to serve more than 4 people, just double the recipe.

Lemony Chicken and Pappardelle

230 g (8 ounces) pappardelle (wide egg noodles)
280 g (10 ounces) frozen sugar snap peas, thawed
400 ml (14 ounces) chicken stock
1 teaspoon fresh, grated lemon peel
2 cups (280 g) cubed, skinless roast chicken meat
½ cup (125 ml) pouring cream

- Cook pasta in large saucepan with boiling water according to package directions, but add snap peas to noodles 1 minute before noodles are done. Drain and return to saucepan.
- Add chicken stock, lemon peel, chicken pieces and ½ teaspoon (2 ml) each of salt and pepper. Heat, stirring constantly, until thoroughly hot.
- Gently stir in pouring cream over low heat. Serve hot. Serves 8.

Lime-Salsa Campsite Chicken

¼ cup (60 ml) oil
280 g (10 ounces) green chilli salsa
1½ tablespoons (25 ml) lime juice
½ teaspoon sugar
1 teaspoon garlic powder
1 teaspoon ground cumin
½ teaspoon oregano
6 boneless, skinless chicken breast halves

- Combine all ingredients except chicken in bowl and mix well. Add chicken breasts and marinate for 3 to 4 hours.
- Barbecue over hot coals for about 10 to 15 minutes or until juices run clear. Turn occasionally. Serves 6.

Mandarin Chicken

300 g (11 ounces) mandarins, peeled and sliced
170 g (6 ounces) orange juice
1 tablespoon (15 ml) lemon juice
1 tablespoon (15 g) cornflour
4 boneless, skinless chicken breast halves
2 tablespoons (20 g) garlic and herb seasoning
2 tablespoons (30 g) butter

- Combine mandarins, orange juice, lemon juice, ⅔ cup (150 ml) water and cornflour in saucepan. Cook on medium heat, stirring constantly, until mixture thickens. Set aside.
- Sprinkle chicken breasts with seasoning and place in frypan with butter. Cook for about 7 minutes on each side until brown.
- Lower heat and spoon orange juice mixture over chicken, cover, simmer for about 20 minutes and add a little water if sauce gets too thick. Serves 4.

Maple-Plum Glazed Turkey Breast

2 cups (640 g) plum jam
1 cup (250 ml) maple syrup
1 teaspoon dry mustard
¼ cup (60 ml) lemon juice
2.2 kg (5 pounds) bone-in turkey breast

- Combine plum jam, syrup, mustard and lemon juice in saucepan and bring to a boil.
- Turn down heat and simmer for about 20 minutes or until glaze is thick. Set aside 1 cup of glaze (250 ml).
- Place turkey breast in roasting pan, pour remaining glaze over turkey and bake according to directions on turkey package.
- Slice turkey and serve with heated, set-aside glaze. Serves 8.

Creamy Chicken and Mushrooms

½ cup (115 g) butter
680 g (1½ pounds) fresh mushrooms, sliced
3 cups (420 g) cooked, cubed chicken
⅓ cup (40 g) flour
800 ml (27 ounces) chicken stock
½ cup (125 ml) sherry
Cayenne pepper

- Melt butter in large frypan over medium-high heat and sauté mushrooms. Add chicken and cook for 3 to 4 minutes. Add flour, stir well to remove lumps and slowly pour in stock while stirring.
- Reduce heat and simmer for about 10 to 15 minutes. Add sherry and cayenne pepper just before serving. Serves 8.

Hurry-Up Chicken Enchiladas

2½–3 cups (350–420 g) cooked, cubed chicken breasts
1 280-g (10-ounce) can cream of chicken soup
1½ cups (395 g) chunky salsa
8 15-cm (6-inch) flour tortillas
200 g processed cheese spread
80 g chilli salsa

- Combine chicken, soup and ½ cup (130 g) chunky salsa in saucepan and heat.
- Spoon about ⅓ cup (50 g) chicken mixture down centre of each tortilla and roll tortilla around filling. Place seam-side down in sprayed 23 x 33-cm (9 x 13-inch) baking dish.
- Mix cheese spread, chilli salsa, remaining chunky salsa and ¼ cup (60 ml) water and pour over enchiladas. Cover with baking paper and microwave on high, turning several times, for 5 minutes. Serves 8.

Mole con Pollo y Arroz

Mole is a traditional Mexican sauce. Chocolate is the secret ingredient used to make the sauce rich, but not overly sweet.

Olive oil
1 cup (160 g) chopped onion
2 cloves garlic, chopped
1 cup (170 g) slivered almonds
30 g (1 ounce) bittersweet chocolate
1 425-g (15-ounce) jar tomato simmer sauce
400 g (14 ounces) chilli salsa
2 cups (280 g) cooked, chopped chicken
1 cup (165 g) cooked rice
Avocado
Lime
Sour cream

- Heat a little oil in frypan and cook onion, garlic and almonds until onions are translucent.
- Add ¼ teaspoon pepper and chocolate and heat on low until chocolate melts. Stir constantly.
- Pour simmer sauce, chilli salsa and chocolate mixture into blender and process until smooth.
- Pour sauce into frypan and add chicken. Mix well and simmer for about 5 to 10 minutes.
- Serve over hot rice and garnish with avocado and lime slices and a dollop of sour cream. Serves 8.

TIP: Mole is a smooth, rich, dark red sauce usually containing a blend of garlic, onion and various chillies and seeds, such as pumpkin seeds. A small amount of chocolate gives the sauce a richer flavour and colour without adding sweetness.

Quick Tex-Mex Dinner

12 corn tortillas
200 g (7 ounces) shredded cheddar cheese
150 g (5 ounces) shredded mozzarella cheese
680 g (1½ pounds) cooked, shredded chicken breast
1 small onion, chopped
560 g (20 ounces) enchilada sauce

- Wrap 6 tortillas in slightly damp paper towel. Place between 2 plates and microwave on high for 30 to 40 seconds.
- Mix cheeses together. On each tortilla, place about ⅓ cup (40 g) cheese, chicken and 1 tablespoon (15 g) onion and roll. Repeat steps with remaining tortillas.
- Place tortillas seam-side down on sprayed 25 x 38-cm (10 x 15-inch) baking dish and pour enchilada sauce on top.
- Sprinkle with remaining cheese and onions, cover and microwave on medium for 5 to 6 minutes. (If microwave does not have turntable, turn tortillas once during cooking.) Serves 8.

Chicken and More

4 boneless, skinless chicken breast halves
Olive oil
2 280-g (10-ounce) cans cream of chicken soup
2 cups (190 g) instant white rice
455 g (16 ounces) frozen broccoli florets

- Brown chicken breasts on both sides in very large frypan with a little oil and simmer for 10 minutes. Remove chicken and keep warm.
- Add soup and 2 cups (500 ml) water. Heat to boiling.
- Stir in instant rice and broccoli florets. Use a little salt and pepper on chicken and place on top of rice. Cover and cook on low for 15 minutes. Serves 4.

Savoury Chicken and Mushrooms

2 red capsicums, chopped
1 brown onion, diced
230 g (8 ounces) mushrooms, sliced
Olive oil
1 280-g (10-ounce) can cream of mushroom soup
1 cup (250 ml) milk
1 roasted chicken, boned
Rice, cooked

- Cook capsicums, onion and mushrooms in large frypan with a little oil for about 5 minutes or until onions are translucent. Stir frequently.
- Stir in mushroom soup and milk, mix well and add chicken pieces and seasonings.
- Boil, reduce heat and cook for about 10 minutes. Serve over rice. Serves 8.

Frypan Chicken and Peas

Olive oil
4–5 boneless, skinless chicken breast halves
2 280-g (10-ounce) cans cream of chicken soup
2 cups (190 g) instant rice
280 g (10 ounces) frozen green peas

- Heat a little oil in very large frypan. Add chicken and cook until it browns well. Transfer chicken to plate and keep warm.
- In same frypan, add soup, 1¾ cups (425 ml) water and about ½ teaspoon pepper. Heat to boiling, stir in rice and peas and reduce heat. Place chicken on top and cook on low heat for 15 minutes. Serves 5.

Frypan Chicken and Stuffing

450 g (16 ounces) frozen corn
¼ cup (115 g) butter
4 boneless, skinless chicken breast halves, cooked
170 g (6 ounces) chicken stuffing mix

- Combine corn, butter and 1⅔ cups (400 ml) water in large frypan and bring to a boil.
- Reduce heat, cover and simmer for 5 minutes.
- Stir in stuffing mix just until moist. Cut chicken into thin slices and mix with stuffing-corn mixture. Cook on low heat just until mixture heats well. Serves 4.

Chicken Piccata

5–6 boneless, skinless chicken breast halves
Flour
Olive oil
3 tablespoons (45 g) butter
1 clove garlic, minced
450 g (1 pound) mushrooms, sliced
400 ml (14 ounces) chicken stock
½ cup (125 ml) dry white wine
1 lemon
2 tablespoons (30 g) capers

- Rinse chicken pieces, pat dry and flatten to about ½ cm (¼ inch) thick with rolling pin. Dredge in flour and coat well.
- Pour a little oil and butter into a large frypan and heat over medium-high heat. Place chicken in frypan and brown on all sides. Remove from pan and keep warm.
- Sauté garlic and mushrooms until tender. Add stock, wine and 3 to 4 tablespoons (45 ml) lemon juice and simmer for several minutes.
- Return chicken to frypan and coat with liquid. Add capers and simmer until chicken is done and juices run clear. Serves 5 to 6.

Southern Fried Chicken

1 whole chicken, cut up
2 eggs, beaten
2 tablespoons (30 ml) cream
Flour
Olive oil or shortening

- Salt and pepper each piece of chicken. Combine beaten eggs and cream in bowl, dip chicken into mixture and roll in flour. Coat chicken well.
- Heat about ½ cm (¼ inch) oil or shortening in heavy frypan and brown chicken on both sides. Lower heat and cook for 25 minutes or until tender.

Gravy:

3 tablespoons (20 g) flour
1½ cups (375 ml) milk

- Remove chicken from frypan and add flour and ½ teaspoon each of salt and pepper. Stir and increase heat to high. Add milk and cook. Stir until gravy thickens. Serve hot. Serves 6.

Stir-Fried Chicken Spaghetti

450 g (1 pound) boneless, skinless chicken breast halves
Olive oil
1½ cups (110 g) sliced mushrooms
1½ cups (140 g) capsicum strips
1 cup (250 ml) sweet-and-sour stir-fry sauce
450 g (16 ounces) spaghetti, cooked
¼ cup (60 g) butter

- Season chicken with salt and pepper and cut into thin slices. Brown chicken slices in large frypan with a little oil and cook for 5 minutes on medium-low heat. Transfer to plate and set aside.
- In same frypan with a little more oil, stir-fry mushrooms and capsicum strips for 5 minutes. Add chicken strips and sweet-and-sour sauce and stir until ingredients are hot.
- Cook pasta according to package directions and drain well. Add butter and stir until butter melts. Place in large bowl and toss with chicken mixture. Serve hot. Serves 5.

Spaghetti Toss

280 g (10 ounces) thin spaghetti
280 g (10 ounces) frozen sugar snap peas
2 tablespoons (45 g) butter
3 cups (420 g) roast chicken
300 g (11 ounces) mandarins, peeled and sliced
⅔ cup (165 ml) stir-fry sauce

- Cook pasta according to package directions. Stir in sugar snap peas and cook for an additional minute.
- Drain and stir in butter until butter melts. Spoon into bowl. Cut chicken into strips and add strips, mandarins and stir-fry sauce. Toss to coat. Serves 8.

Chicken Kick

1 tablespoon (15 g) paprika
1 teaspoon ground cumin
½ teaspoon cayenne pepper
½ teaspoon coriander
½ teaspoon oregano
4–5 boneless, skinless chicken breasts, halved lengthwise
Extra-virgin olive oil

- Combine paprika, cumin, cayenne pepper, coriander, oregano and 1 teaspoon salt in small bowl.
- Place chicken pieces in large shallow baking dish and drizzle with olive oil to coat. Rub each piece with spice mix and let stand for about 10 minutes.
- Brown chicken pieces in large frypan over medium-high heat. Reduce heat, cover and simmer for about 10 minutes on each side. Transfer to serving platter. Serves 6 to 8.

Honey-Glazed Chicken

4 skinless chicken breast halves
Canola oil
1 625-g (22-ounce) can pineapple chunks with juice
½ cup (125 g) honey-mustard dressing
1 green capsicum, thinly sliced
1 red capsicum, thinly sliced
280 g (10 ounces) couscous, cooked

- Cut chicken into strips, add a little salt and pepper and brown in large frypan with a little oil.
- Add juice from pineapple, cover and simmer for 15 minutes.
- Add honey-mustard dressing, capsicum slices and pineapple chunks to chicken. Bring to a boil, reduce heat, cover and simmer for additional 15 minutes. Serve over couscous. Serves 4.

Stir-Fried Chicken

Olive oil
450 g (1 pound) chicken tenderloins, cut into strips
450 g (16 ounces) frozen broccoli, cauliflower and carrots
230 g (8 ounces) stir-fry sauce
340 g (12 ounces) chow mein noodles

- Place a little oil and stir-fry chicken strips in 30-cm (12-inch) wok over high heat for about 4 minutes.
- Add vegetables and stir-fry for an additional 4 minutes or until vegetables are tender. Stir in stir-fry sauce and cook just until mixture is hot. Serve over chow mein noodles. Serves 8.

Sunny Chicken

4 boneless, skinless chicken breast halves
1½ teaspoons curry powder
1½ cups (375 ml) orange juice
1 tablespoon (15 g) brown sugar
1 cup (95 g) rice
1 teaspoon mustard

- Rub chicken with curry powder and a little salt and pepper. Combine orange juice, brown sugar, rice and mustard in large frypan and mix well.
- Place chicken on top of rice mixture and bring to a boil. Reduce heat, cover and simmer for 30 minutes. Remove from heat and let stand, covered, for about 10 minutes until all liquid absorbs into rice. Serves 4.

Sweet 'n' Spicy Chicken

450 g (1 pound) boneless, skinless chicken breast halves
1 30-g (1-ounce) packet taco seasoning
Olive oil
450 g (16 ounces) chunky salsa
1 cup (320 g) peach jam
Rice or noodles, cooked

- Cut chicken into 1-cm (½-inch) cubes. Place chicken in large, resealable plastic bag, add taco seasoning and toss to coat.
- Brown chicken in frypan with a little oil. Combine salsa and jam in bowl, stir into frypan and bring mixture to a boil.
- Reduce heat, cover and simmer until juices run clear. Serve over rice or noodles. Serves 4.

Tempting Chicken

3 boneless, skinless chicken breast halves
3 boneless, skinless chicken thighs
Olive oil
1 455-g (16-ounce) jar tomato-alfredo sauce
1 280-g (10-ounce) can cream of tomato soup

- Brown chicken pieces in large frypan with a little oil.
- Heat tomato-alfredo sauce, tomato soup and ½ cup (125 ml) water in saucepan just enough to mix. Pour over chicken.
- Cover and simmer for about 30 minutes. Serves 6.

Tasty Frypan Chicken

5 large boneless, skinless chicken breast halves
Olive oil
1 green capsicum, julienned
1 red capsicum, julienned
2 small yellow squash, julienned
450 g (16 ounces) thick-and-chunky salsa
Rice, cooked

- Cut chicken breasts into thin strips. Sauté chicken in large frypan with a little oil for about 5 minutes. Add capsicums and squash and cook for an additional 5 minutes or until capsicums are tender but crisp.
- Stir in salsa and bring to a boil, lower heat and simmer for 10 minutes. Serve over rice. Serves 5.

Tequila-Lime Chicken

½ cup (125 ml) lime juice
¼ cup (60 ml) tequila
1½ teaspoons chilli powder
1½ teaspoons minced garlic
1 teaspoon seeded jalapeno chilli, sliced
6 boneless, chicken breast halves with skin

- Combine all ingredients except chicken in large resealable plastic bag. Add chicken, seal bag and turn to coat. Refrigerate for 10 hours or overnight.
- Remove chicken from marinade and sprinkle chicken with a little salt and pepper. Discard marinade.
- Barbecue or fry skin-side down for 5 to 7 minutes. Turn and barbecue for 10 minutes or until it cooks thoroughly. Remove to platter, cover and let stand for 5 minutes before serving. Serves 6.

Turkey-Asparagus Alfredo

1 bunch fresh asparagus
1 red capsicum, julienned
1 455-g (16-ounce) jar alfredo sauce
230 g (½ pound) smoked turkey, cut into strips

- Bring ½ cup (125 ml) water to boil in large frypan. Cut off woody ends of asparagus and cut into thirds. Add asparagus and capsicum to frypan, cook on medium-high heat for 4 minutes or until tender but crisp and drain.
- Stir in alfredo sauce and turkey strips. Bring to a boil, reduce heat and simmer until mixture is thoroughly hot. Serves 6.

Tortellini Dinner

1 255-g (9-ounce) package refrigerated cheese tortellini
280 g (10 ounces) frozen green peas, thawed
230 g (8 ounces) cream cheese with chives
½ cup (120 g) sour cream
250 g (9 ounces) cooked chicken breasts

- Cook pasta in saucepan according to package directions. Place peas in colander and pour hot pasta water over green peas. Return pasta and peas to saucepan.
- Combine cream cheese and sour cream in smaller saucepan and heat on low, stirring well until cheese melts. Spoon mixture over pasta and peas and toss with heat on low.
- Heat cooked chicken in microwave. Spoon pasta and peas in serving bowl and place chicken on top. Serve hot. Serves 6.

Q: Why didn't the chicken skeleton cross the road?

A: Because he didn't have enough guts.

Texas Chicken Fajitas

6 boneless, skinless chicken breast halves
Flour tortillas
1 cup (265 g) salsa
1 cup (250 ml) Italian salad dressing
2 tablespoons (30 ml) lemon juice
2 tablespoons (20 g) chopped spring onions
1 teaspoon garlic powder
1 teaspoon celery salt
Salsa
Guacamole
Grilled onions
Chopped tomatoes
Grated cheese
Sour cream

- Combine salsa, dressing, lemon juice, spring onions, garlic and celery salt with 1 teaspoon pepper into a bowl and mix well. Remove fat from meat and wipe dry with paper towels.
- Place meat in shallow dish and pour marinade over meat. Marinate overnight or for at least 6 hours in refrigerator.
- Drain liquid and cook over hot charcoal. Cut meat diagonally. Place a few meat strips on warmed flour tortilla, choose fillings, roll and eat! Serves 8.

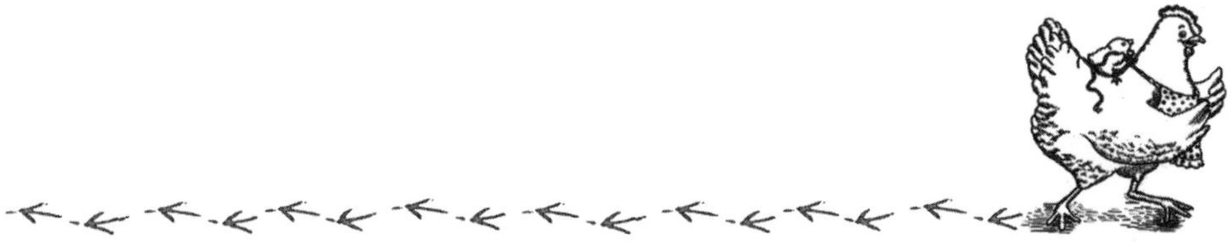

Turkey Croquettes

These are very easy to make. Make several batches and freeze them for another meal.

1½ cups (210 g) cooked, chopped turkey
1 280-g (10-ounce) can cream of chicken soup
1 cup (35 g) turkey stuffing mix
2 eggs
1 tablespoon (10 g) minced onion
Flour
Canola oil

- Mix all ingredients in bowl and refrigerate for several hours. Shape into patties or rolls. Dredge in flour and fry in deep oil until brown. Serves 6.

Wild Rice and Chicken

170 g (6 ounces) mixed long grain and wild rice
4 boneless, skinless chicken breast halves
½ cup (115 g) butter
1 large red capsicum, chopped

- Prepare rice according to package directions.
- Cook chicken in 2 tablespoons (30 g) butter in large frypan and make sure each chicken breast browns on both sides. Remove chicken and keep warm.
- Add remaining butter to pan drippings and sauté capsicum until tender. Add to rice. Serve with cooked chicken breasts. Serves 4.

Chicken and Rice Olé

This may be served as a 1-dish meal or as a sandwich wrapped in flour tortillas.

450 g (1 pound) chicken mince
1 155-g (5½-ounce) package Spanish rice mix
1 425-g (15-ounce) can black beans or borlotti beans, rinsed and drained
1 cup (265 g) thick-and-chunky salsa

- Brown mince in large frypan and break up large pieces with fork. Add rice mix and 2 cups (500 ml) water.
- Bring to a boil, reduce heat and simmer for about 8 minutes or until rice is tender. Stir in beans and salsa and cook just until mixture is hot. Serves 6.

Dad's Best Smoked Chicken

3 whole chickens, cut in half, or an equivalent amount of smoked chicken
½ cup (115 g) butter
2 teaspoons Worcestershire sauce
2 dashes Tabasco sauce
2 tablespoons (30 ml) lemon juice
½ teaspoon garlic salt
1 375-ml (12-ounce) can lemon-lime soft drink

- Sprinkle chickens with pepper and leave at room temperature for 1 hour. Melt butter in small saucepan and add Worcestershire sauce, Tabasco sauce, lemon juice, garlic salt and carbonated drink.
- If you are smoking your own chickens, cook chickens over low charcoal fire with hickory or mesquite chips around sides of fire. Turn often and baste with sauce mixture several times. If you are using smoked chicken, cook in a barbecue with the lid closed, basting several times.
- When chicken is done (about 60 minutes), baste once more to keep chicken moist. Serves 12.

Yummy Barbecue-Grilled Chicken

6 boneless, skinless chicken breast halves
3 cups (815 g) tomato sauce
½ cup (110 g) packed brown sugar
¼ cup (60 ml) Worcestershire sauce
2 tablespoons (30 ml) vinegar
1 teaspoon chilli sauce

- Wash chicken and dry with paper towels. Combine tomato sauce, brown sugar, Worcestershire sauce, vinegar, 2 teaspoons salt, chilli sauce and ½ teaspoon pepper in saucepan and mix well.
- Bring to a boil, reduce heat to low and cook for 15 minutes.
- Fire up barbecue and smoke chicken over hickory wood, if possible. Baste chicken frequently with barbecue sauce. Turn chicken periodically and cook chicken 8 to 10 minutes per side or until juices are clear.
- Any leftover barbecue sauce keeps well in refrigerator. Serves 6.

When using the barbecue, clean the hotplates well before each use to prevent bacterial contamination.

Texas-Pecan Chicken

1 cup (250 ml) buttermilk*
1 egg, beaten
1 cup (120 g) flour
1 cup (110 g) very finely grated pecans
2 tablespoons (15 g) sesame seeds
2 teaspoons paprika
6–8 boneless, skinless, chicken breast halves
¼ cup (60 g) butter
½ cup (55 g) chopped pecans

- Preheat oven to 175° C (350° F).
- Combine buttermilk and egg in shallow bowl.
- In separate bowl, combine flour, grated pecans, sesame seeds, paprika, 1 teaspoon salt and ¼ teaspoon pepper.
- Dip chicken breasts in egg-milk mixture and coat well in flour-pecan mixture.
- Melt butter in large baking dish and place breaded chicken in pan. Sprinkle chopped pecans over chicken breasts.
- Bake for 30 to 35 minutes or until flour mixture is light brown. Serves 8.

*TIP: *To make buttermilk, mix 1 cup (250 ml) milk with 1 tablespoon (15 ml) lemon juice or vinegar and let milk rest for about 10 minutes.*

Chicken Tarragon

Tarragon works wonders for this chicken.

1 230-g (8-ounce) package fettuccini (egg noodles)
1 cup (250 ml) dry white wine
1 teaspoon dried tarragon leaves
1 30-g (1-ounce) packet dry vegetable soup mix
4 boneless, skinless chicken breast halves
230 g (8 ounces) sour cream

- Cook pasta according to package directions, drain and set aside. Pour 2 cups (500 ml) water into large frypan. Over medium heat add wine and tarragon and bring to boil. Stir in dry soup mix and boil for 5 minutes.
- Add chicken and reduce heat. Cover and simmer for 15 minutes or until juices run clear. Arrange noodles on serving dish. Use slotted spoon to remove chicken, place on top of noodles and cover with foil.
- Boil juices in frypan for about 5 to 10 minutes or until liquid reduces to ½ cup (125 ml). Turn heat to low and stir constantly while adding sour cream. Heat for 3 to 4 minutes more and pour over chicken. Serves 4.

Slow Clucker

Pluck a little oregano here, stir in some veggies there, throw in some chicken and let your slow cooker do all the work! Over 60 savoury chicken recipes allow you to add ingredients to the cooker, go about your busy day and come home to a warm, wonderful dinner sure to please your flock.

Slow Clucker Contents

Arroz con Pollo

1.4 kg (3 pounds) chicken thighs
2 425-g (15-ounce) cans Italian tomatoes
450 g (16 ounces) frozen green peas, thawed
2 cups (370 g) long grain rice
1 10-g (⅓-ounce) packet yellow rice seasoning mix
800 ml (27 ounces) chicken stock
1 heaped teaspoon minced garlic
1 teaspoon dried oregano

- Combine all ingredients plus ¾ cup (175 ml) water in sprayed slow cooker and stir well.
- Cover and cook on low for 7 to 8 hours or on high for 3 hours 30 minutes to 4 hours. Serves 10.

Bacon-Wrapped Fiesta Chicken

6 boneless, skinless chicken breast halves
6 slices bacon
2 280-g (10-ounce) cans mushroom soup
½ teaspoon beef stock
170 g (6 ounces) rice, cooked
Parmesan cheese, grated butter

- Roll each chicken breast in slice of bacon and place in a 5-L (5-quart) slow cooker.
- Pour mushroom soup and ⅓ cup (75 ml) water in saucepan, heat just enough to mix and pour over chicken. Cover and cook on low for 7 to 8 hours. Serve over rice mixed with cheese and butter. Serves 6.

Artichoke and Chicken Pasta

680 g (1½ pounds) boneless chicken breast tenders
1 425-g (15-ounce) jar artichoke hearts, quartered
¾ cup (110 g) roasted red capsicums, chopped
230 g (8 ounces) tasty cheese, shredded
1 tablespoon (15 ml) Worcestershire sauce
1 280-g (10-ounce) can cream of chicken soup
230 g (8 ounces) shredded cheddar cheese
4 cups (300 g) hot, cooked bow-tie pasta

- Combine chicken, artichoke, roasted red capsicum, cheese, Worcestershire sauce and soup in slow cooker and mix well.
- Cover and cook on low for 6 to 8 hours. About 20 minutes before serving, fold in cheddar cheese, hot pasta, and a little salt and pepper. Serves 8.

Cooked chicken should not be left out of the refrigerator longer than two hours.

Broccoli and Rice Chicken

1¼ cups (120 g) rice
900 g (2 pounds) boneless, skinless chicken breast halves
1 teaspoon dried parsley
1 45-g (1½-ounce) packet cream of broccoli soup mix
400 g (14 ounces) chicken stock

- Place rice in lightly sprayed slow cooker. Cut chicken into slices and put over rice.
- Sprinkle with parsley.
- Combine soup mix, chicken stock and 1 cup (250 ml) water in saucepan. Heat just enough to mix well. Pour over chicken and rice.
- Cover and cook on low for 6 to 8 hours. Serves 8.

Stuffy Chicken

This is a great recipe for leftover chicken.

1 280-g (10-ounce) can cream of chicken soup
2 sticks celery, sliced
½ cup (115 g) butter, melted
3 cups (420 g) cooked, cubed chicken
450 g (16 ounces) frozen broccoli, corn and capsicum
230 g (8 ounces) stuffing mix

- Combine chicken soup, celery, butter, cubed chicken, vegetables, stuffing mix and ⅓ cup (75 ml) water in large saucepan and heat just enough to mix well.
- Transfer to sprayed 5 to 6-L (5 to 6-quart) slow cooker. Cover and cook on low for 5 to 6 hours. Serves 8.

Chicken Alfredo

680 g (1½ pounds) boneless, skinless chicken thighs
2 sticks celery, sliced diagonally
1 red capsicum, julienned
1 455-g (16-ounce) jar alfredo sauce
3 cups (215 g) fresh broccoli florets
1 230-g (8-ounce) package fettuccini or linguine
145 g (5 ounces) grated parmesan cheese

- Cut chicken into strips. Layer chicken, celery and capsicum in 4 to 5-L (4 to 5-quart) slow cooker. Pour alfredo sauce evenly over vegetables. Cover and cook on low for 5 to 6 hours.
- About 30 minutes before serving, turn heat to high and add broccoli to chicken-alfredo mixture. Cover and cook for an additional 30 minutes. Serves 8.
- Cook pasta according to package directions and drain. Just before serving, pour pasta into cooker, mix and sprinkle parmesan cheese on top.

Chicken Meets Italy

450 g (16 ounces) frozen whole green beans, thawed
1 onion, chopped
1 cup (70 g) halved fresh mushrooms
3 boneless, skinless chicken breast halves
1 425-g (15-ounce) can Italian tomatoes
1 teaspoon chicken stock powder
1 teaspoon minced garlic
1 teaspoon Italian seasoning
230 g (8 ounces) fettuccini
145 g (5 ounces) parmesan cheese

- Place green beans, onion and mushrooms in sprayed 4 to 5-L (4 to 5-quart) slow cooker. Cut chicken into 2-cm (1-inch) pieces and place over vegetables.
- Combine tomatoes, chicken stock, garlic and Italian seasoning in small bowl. Pour over chicken. Cover and cook on low for 5 to 6 hours.
- Cook fettuccini according to package directions and drain. Serve chicken over fettuccini and sprinkle with parmesan cheese. Serves 6.

TIP: For added flavour, you can add ¼ cup (60 g) butter.

Chicken and Everything Good

2 280-g (10-ounce) cans cream of chicken soup
⅓ cup (75 g) butter, melted
3 cups (420 g) cooked, cubed chicken
450 g (16 ounces) frozen broccoli florets, corn and red capsicum
280 g (10 ounces) frozen green peas
230 g (8 ounces) stuffing mix

- Combine soup, melted butter and ⅓ cup (75 ml) water in large saucepan; heat just enough to mix well.
- Add chicken, vegetables and stuffing mix and stir well. Spoon mixture into sprayed slow cooker. Cover and cook on low for 5 to 6 hours or on high for 3 hours. Serves 8.

Chicken-in-the-Garden

4–5 boneless, skinless chicken breast halves
450 g (16 ounces) frozen broccoli, cauliflower and carrots, thawed
1 280-g (10-ounce) can cream of celery soup
230 g (8 ounces) shredded cheddar cheese, divided

- Cut chicken into strips and place chicken strips sprinkled with 2 teaspoons salt in sprayed slow cooker.
- Combine vegetables, celery soup and half cheese in saucepan and heat just enough to mix well. Spoon over chicken breasts.
- Cover and cook on low for 4 to 5 hours. About 10 minutes before serving, sprinkle remaining cheese on top of casserole. Serves 6.

Chicken Curry over Rice

3 boneless, skinless chicken breast halves
½ cup (125 ml) chicken stock
1 280-g (10-ounce) can cream of chicken soup
1 onion, coarsely chopped
1 red capsicum, cut into strips
¼ cup (40 g) sultanas
1½ teaspoons curry powder
¼ teaspoon ground ginger
Rice, cooked

- Cut chicken into thin strips.
- Combine chicken strips, stock, soup, onion, capsicum, sultanas, curry powder and ginger in saucepan, just enough to mix well.
- Pour into sprayed 5 to 6-L (5 to 6-quart) slow cooker, cover and cook on low for 3 to 4 hours. Serve over rice. Serves 4.

Chicken Sherry

5–6 boneless skinless chicken breast halves
450 g (16 ounces) frozen broccoli florets, thawed
1 red capsicum, julienned
1 455-g (16-ounce) jar mixed cheese pasta sauce
3 tablespoons (45 ml) sherry
Pasta, cooked

- Brown chicken in frypan and place in sprayed oval 5 to 6-L (5 to 6-quart) slow cooker.
- Place broccoli on plate, remove stems and discard.
- Combine broccoli, capsicum, cheese sauce and sherry in bowl and mix well. Spoon over chicken breasts.
- Cover and cook on low for 4 to 5 hours. Serve over pasta. Serves 6.

Chicken Breast Deluxe

4 slices bacon
5–6 boneless, skinless chicken breast halves
1 cup (100 g) sliced celery
1 cup (150 g) sliced red capsicum
1 280-g (10-ounce) can cream of chicken soup
2 tablespoons (30 ml) white wine or cooking wine
6 slices Swiss cheese
2 tablespoons (5 g) dried parsley

- Cook bacon in large frypan, drain, crumble and set aside drippings.
- Place chicken in frypan with bacon drippings and lightly brown on both sides.
- Transfer chicken to sprayed slow cooker and place celery and red capsicum over chicken.
- In same frypan, combine soup and wine, heat just enough to mix well and spoon over vegetables and chicken in slow cooker. Cover and cook on low for 3 to 4 hours.
- Top with slices of cheese over each chicken breast, sprinkle with parsley and cook for an additional 10 minutes.
- When serving, sprinkle crumbled bacon over each serving. Serves 6.

Coq au Vin

4 chicken quarters
Olive oil
10–12 small white onions, peeled
230 g (½ pound) whole button mushrooms
1 teaspoon minced garlic
½ teaspoon dried thyme leaves
10–12 small new (red) potatoes with skin on
280 g (10 ounces) chicken stock
1 cup (250 ml) red wine
6 slices bacon, cooked, crumbled

- Brown chicken quarters in frypan with oil on both sides and set aside.
- Place white onions, whole mushrooms, garlic and thyme in slow cooker.
- Add chicken quarters, potatoes, chicken stock and a little salt and pepper.
- Cover and cook on low for 8 to 10 hours or on high for 3 to 4 hours.
- During last hour, turn heat to high, add wine and continue cooking.
- Sprinkle crumbled bacon over chicken before serving. Serves 4 to 6.

Veggie-Chicken Dinner

5–6 boneless, skinless chicken breast halves
6 carrots, cut in 2-cm (1-inch) lengths
1 425-g (15-ounce) can cut green beans, drained
1 425-g (15-ounce) can whole new potatoes, drained
2 280-g (10-ounce) cans cream of mushroom soup
Shredded cheddar cheese

- Wash chicken breasts and dry with paper towel. Place in sprayed slow cooker.
- Combine carrots, green beans, potatoes and mushroom soup in saucepan, heat just enough to mix well and pour over chicken in cooker.
- Cover and cook on low for 8 to 10 hours. When ready to serve, sprinkle cheese on top. Serves 6.

Q: Which side of a chicken has the most feathers?

A: The outside.

Chicken-Celery Delight

¾ cup (120 g) cooked white rice
400 ml (14 ounces) chicken stock
1 30-g (1-ounce) packet onion soup mix
1 red capsicum, seeded and chopped
2 280-g (10-ounce) cans cream of celery soup
¾ cup (175 ml) white cooking wine
4–6 boneless, skinless chicken breast halves
145 g (5 ounces) grated parmesan cheese

- Combine rice, stock, soup mix, capsicum, celery soup, ¾ cup (175 ml) water, wine and several sprinkles of black pepper in saucepan and heat just enough to mix well.
- Place chicken breasts in sprayed 6-L (6-quart) oval slow cooker. Pour rice-soup mixture over chicken breasts. Cover and cook on low for 4 to 6 hours.
- One hour before serving, sprinkle parmesan cheese over chicken. Serves 6.

Whole Lotta Chicken Dinner

1 cup (95 g) rice
1 tablespoon (15 g) chicken seasoning
1 30-g (1-ounce) packet onion soup mix
1 green capsicum, seeded, chopped
115 g (4 ounces) diced roasted red capsicum
¾ teaspoon dried basil
400 ml (14 ounces) chicken stock
1 280-g (10-ounce) can cream of chicken soup
5–6 boneless, skinless chicken breast halves

- Combine rice, chicken seasoning, onion soup mix, capsicum, roasted red capsicum, basil, stock, ½ cup (125 ml) water and chicken soup in saucepan and heat just enough to mix well.
- Place chicken in sprayed slow cooker and cover chicken with rice mixture. Cover and cook on low for 6 to 7 hours. Serves 6.

Q: Why couldn't the chicken find her eggs?

A: Because she mislaid them.

Chicken for the Gods

1¾ cups (210 g) flour
2 tablespoons (20 g) dry mustard
6 boneless, skinless chicken breast halves
2 tablespoons (30 ml) olive oil
1 280-g (10-ounce) can chicken soup

- Place flour and mustard in shallow bowl and dredge chicken breasts.
- Brown chicken in frypan with oil. Place all breasts in sprayed 6-L (6-quart) slow cooker.
- Pour chicken soup over chicken and add about ¼ (60 ml) cup water.
- Cover and cook on low for 6 to 7 hours. Serves 6.

Stuffed Chicken-Ready Dinner

170 g (6 ounces) chicken stuffing mix
3 cups (420 g) cooked, chopped chicken breast halves
450 g (16 ounces) frozen whole green beans, thawed
650 ml (23 ounces) chicken gravy

- Prepare stuffing mix according to package directions and place in sprayed slow cooker.
- Follow with layer of chopped chicken breasts and place green beans over chicken. Pour chicken gravy over green beans.
- Cover and cook on low for 3 hours 30 minutes to 4 hours 30 minutes. Serves 8.

Cream Cheese Chicken

4 boneless, skinless chicken breast halves
2 tablespoons (30 g) butter, melted
1 280-g (10-ounce) can cream of mushroom soup
1 10-g (½-ounce) packet Italian seasoning mix
½ cup (125 ml) sherry
230 g (8 ounces) cream cheese, cubed
Pasta, cooked

- Wash chicken breasts, dry with paper towels, brush melted butter over chicken and place in sprayed slow cooker. Add remaining ingredients to saucepan, heat just enough to mix well and add to slow cooker.
- Cover and cook on low for 6 to 7 hours. Serve over hot pasta. Serves 4.

Creamy Chicken and Potatoes

4 boneless, skinless chicken breast halves
2 teaspoons chicken seasoning
8–10 small new (red) potatoes with skin on
1 280-g (10-ounce) can cream of chicken soup
230 g (8 ounces) sour cream

- Place chicken breast halves, sprinkled with chicken seasoning, in slow cooker. Arrange new potatoes around chicken.
- Combine soup, sour cream and lots of pepper in saucepan and heat just enough to mix well. Spoon over chicken breasts. Cover and cook on low for 4 to 6 hours. Serves 4.

Happy Hearty Chicken

4–5 carrots, peeled
6 medium new (red) potatoes with skin on, quartered
4–5 boneless, skinless chicken breast halves
1 tablespoon (15 g) chicken seasoning
2 280-g (10-ounce) cans cream of chicken soup
⅓ cup (85 ml) white wine or cooking wine

- Cut carrots into 1-cm (½-inch) pieces. Place potatoes and carrots in slow cooker. Sprinkle chicken breasts with chicken seasoning and place over vegetables.
- Heat soup with ¼ cup (60 ml) water and wine in saucepan, just enough to mix well and pour over chicken and vegetables. Cover and cook on low for 5 to 6 hours. Serves 5.

TIP: For a tasty change, use 1 280-g (10-ounce) can chicken soup and 1 280-g (10-ounce) can mushroom soup instead of cream of chicken soup.

Chicken with Orange Sauce

1 whole chicken, quartered
½ cup (60 g) plus 2 tablespoons (20 g) flour
½ teaspoon ground nutmeg
½ teaspoon ground cinnamon
2 large sweet potatoes, peeled, sliced
1 230-g (8-ounce) can pineapple chunks with juice
1 280-g (10-ounce) can cream of chicken soup
⅔ cup (165 ml) orange juice
Rice, cooked

- Wash chicken quarters and dry with paper towels. Combine ½ cup (60 g) flour, nutmeg and cinnamon in bowl and coat chicken. Place sweet potatoes and pineapple in large sprayed slow cooker. Arrange chicken on top.
- Combine chicken soup, orange juice and remaining flour in saucepan, heat just enough to mix well and pour over chicken. Cover and cook on low for 7 to 9 hours or on high for 3 to 4 hours. Serve over hot rice. Serves 6.

Chow Mein Chicken

4 boneless, skinless chicken breast halves
2–3 cups sliced celery
1 onion, coarsely chopped
¼ cup (60 ml) soy sauce
¼ teaspoon cayenne pepper
400 ml (14 ounces) chicken stock
300 g (11 ounces) bean shoots
1 230-g (8-ounce) can water chestnuts, drained
1 425-g (15-ounce) can bamboo shoots
¼ cup (30 g) flour
170 g (6 ounces) chow mein noodles

- Combine chicken, celery, onion, soy sauce, cayenne pepper and chicken stock in sprayed slow cooker. Cover and cook on low for 3 to 4 hours.
- Add bean shoots, water chestnuts and bamboo shoots to chicken.
- Mix flour and ¼ cup (60 ml) water and stir into chicken and vegetables. Cook an additional 1 hour.
- Serve over noodles. Serves 4.

Creamed Chicken and Vegetables

1 280-g (10-ounce) can cream of chicken soup
4 large boneless, skinless chicken breast halves, sliced thinly
450 g (16 ounces) frozen peas and carrots, thawed
340 g (12 ounces) chicken gravy

- Pour soup and ½ cup (125 ml) water into sprayed 6-L (6-quart) slow cooker.
- Mix and add chicken slices. Sprinkle a little salt and lots of pepper over chicken and soup.
- Cover and cook on low for 4 to 5 hours.
- Add peas and carrots, chicken gravy and ½ cup (125 ml) water. Increase heat to high and cook for about 1 hour or until peas and carrots are tender. Serves 6.

TIP: *Serve over large buttermilk scones or over thick toast.*

The record for laying the most eggs in a day is seven eggs.

Creamed Chicken

4 large boneless, skinless chicken breast halves
Lemon juice
1 red capsicum, chopped
2 sticks celery, sliced diagonally
1 280-g (10-ounce) can cream of chicken soup
1 280-g (10-ounce) can cream of celery soup
⅓ cup (85 ml) dry white wine
145 g (5 ounces) grated parmesan cheese
Rice, cooked

- Wash chicken and pat dry with paper towels. Rub a little lemon juice over chicken and sprinkle with salt and pepper. Place in slow cooker and top with capsicum and celery.
- Combine soups and wine in saucepan and heat just enough to mix thoroughly. Pour over chicken breasts and sprinkle with parmesan cheese.
- Cover and cook on low for 6 to 7 hours. Serve over buttered rice. Serves 4.

Creamy Salsa Chicken

4–5 boneless, skinless chicken breast halves
1 30-g (1-ounce) packet taco seasoning mix
1 cup (265 g) salsa
½ cup (240 g) sour cream

- Place chicken in 5 to 6-L (5 to 6-quart) slow cooker and add ¼ cup (60 ml) water.
- Sprinkle taco seasoning mix over chicken and top with salsa. Cook on low for 5 to 6 hours.
- When ready to serve, remove chicken and place on platter. Stir sour cream into juices and spoon over chicken breasts. Serves 5.

Delightful Chicken and Veggies

4–5 boneless skinless, chicken breast halves
1 425-g (15-ounce) can corn, drained
280 g (10 ounces) frozen green peas, thawed
1 455-g (16-ounce) jar alfredo sauce
1 teaspoon chicken seasoning
1 teaspoon minced garlic
Pasta, cooked

- Brown chicken in frypan and place in sprayed slow cooker.
- Combine corn, peas, alfredo sauce, ¼ cup (60 ml) water, chicken seasoning and minced garlic in bowl and pour over chicken breasts.
- Cover and cook on low for 4 to 5 hours. Serve over pasta. Serves 5.

Delicious Chicken Pasta

450 g (1 pound) chicken tenderloins
Chicken seasoning
3 tablespoons (45 g) butter
1 onion, coarsely chopped
1 425-g (15-ounce) can diced tomatoes
1 280-g (10-ounce) can mushroom soup
½ teaspoon beef stock powder
230 g (8 ounces) angel hair pasta

- Pat chicken dry with several paper towels and sprinkle with ample amount of chicken seasoning.
- Melt butter in large frypan, brown chicken and place in oval slow cooker. Pour remaining butter over chicken and cover with onion.
- In separate bowl, combine diced tomatoes, mushroom soup and beef stock and pour over chicken and onions. Cover and cook on low for 4 to 5 hours.
- When ready to serve, cook pasta according to package directions. Serve chicken and sauce over pasta. Serves 8.

Easy Slow-Cooked Chicken

5 boneless, skinless chicken breast halves
2 280-g (10-ounce) cans cream of chicken soup
170 g (6 ounces) chicken stuffing mix
450 g (16 ounces) frozen green peas, thawed

- Place chicken in 6-L (6-quart) slow cooker and spoon soup over chicken.
- Combine stuffing mix with ingredients according to package directions; include seasoning packet in bowl and spoon over chicken and soup.
- Cover and cook on low for 5 to 6 hours.
- Sprinkle peas over top of stuffing. Cover and cook for an additional 45 to 50 minutes. Serves 5.

The greatest number of yolks in one chicken egg is nine.

Farmhouse Dinner

230 g (8 ounces) medium spaghetti
4–5 boneless, skinless chicken breast halves
400 ml (14 ounces) chicken stock
2 cups (200 g) sliced celery
2 onions, chopped
1 green capsicum, seeded, chopped
1 red capsicum, seeded, chopped
1 280-g (10-ounce) can cream of chicken soup
1 280-g (10-ounce) can cream of mushroom soup
1 cup (115 g) shredded cheddar

- Cook pasta in boiling water until barely tender and drain well. Cut chicken into thin slices.
- Combine pasta, chicken and stock in large, sprayed slow cooker and mix. (Make sure pasta separates and coats with stock.)
- Combine remaining ingredients in saucepan and heat just enough to mix well and add to slow cooker. Cover and cook on low for 4 to 6 hours. Serves 5.

Golden Chicken Dinner

5 skinless chicken breast halves
6 medium new (red) potatoes with skin on, cubed
6 medium carrots, peeled and quartered
1 tablespoon (2 g) dried parsley flakes
1 280-g (10-ounce) can mushroom soup
1 280-g (10-ounce) can cream of chicken soup
4 tablespoons (15 g) dried mashed potato flakes

- Cut chicken into 1-cm (½-inch) pieces.
- Place potatoes and carrots in slow cooker and top with chicken. Sprinkle parsley flakes, 1 teaspoon salt and a little pepper over chicken.
- Mix soups in bowl and spread over chicken. Cover and slow cook on low for 6 to 7 hours.
- Combine potato flakes and a little water or milk in bowl, mix to make gravy and cook for additional 30 minutes. Serves 8.

Imperial Chicken

1 tablespoon (10 g) Oriental seasoning
170 g (6 ounces) mixed long grain and wild rice
1 455-g (16-ounce) jar roasted garlic and parmesan pasta sauce
6 boneless, skinless chicken breast halves
450 g (16 ounces) frozen green beans, thawed
½ cup (85 g) slivered almonds, toasted

- Pour 2½ cups (625 ml) water, seasoning and rice into sprayed slow cooker and stir well.
- Spoon in pasta sauce and mix well. Place chicken breasts in slow cooker and cover with green beans. Cover and cook on low for 3 to 5 hours.
- When ready to serve, sprinkle with slivered almonds. Serves 6.

Orange Chicken

6 boneless, skinless chicken breast halves
1½ cups (480 g) orange marmalade
250 ml (8 ounces) Thousand Island salad dressing
1 30-g (1-ounce) packet onion soup mix

- Place chicken breasts in slow cooker. Combine orange marmalade, salad dressing, soup mix and ¾ cup (175 ml) water in bowl and stir well.
- Spoon mixture over chicken breasts. Cover and cook on low for 4 to 6 hours. Serves 6.

Italian Chicken

1 small head cabbage
1 onion
1 115-g (4-ounce) jar sliced mushrooms, drained
1 medium zucchini, sliced
1 red capsicum, julienned
1 teaspoon Italian seasoning
680 g (1½ pounds) skinless chicken thighs
1 teaspoon minced garlic
2 425-g (15-ounce) cans Italian tomatoes

- Cut cabbage into wedges, slice onions and separate into rings. Make layers of cabbage, onion, mushrooms, zucchini and capsicum in sprayed 6-L (6-quart) slow cooker.
- Sprinkle Italian seasoning over vegetables. Place chicken thighs on top of vegetables.
- Mix garlic with tomatoes in bowl and pour over chicken. Cover and cook on low for 4 to 6 hours. Serves 6.

TIP: When serving, sprinkle a little parmesan cheese over each serving.

Mushroom Chicken

4 boneless, skinless chicken breast halves
1 425-g (15-ounce) jar tomato simmer sauce
2 115-g (4-ounce) cans sliced mushrooms, drained
200 g (7 ounces) red capsicum, diced
80 g (3 ounces) onion, diced
2 teaspoons Italian seasoning
1 teaspoon minced garlic

- Brown chicken in frypan and place in sprayed slow cooker.
- Combine simmer sauce, mushrooms, capsicums, onions, Italian seasoning, minced garlic and ¼ cup (60 ml) water in bowl and spoon over chicken breasts.
- Cover and cook on low for 4 to 5 hours. Serves 4.

Diner: Do you serve chicken here?

Waiter: Sit down, sir. We serve anyone.

Quick-Fix Chicken

4–6 boneless, skinless chicken breast halves
230 g (8 ounces) sour cream
¼ cup (60 ml) soy sauce
2 280-g (10-ounce) cans French onion soup

- Wash chicken and dry with paper towels. Place in sprayed slow cooker.
- Combine sour cream, soy sauce and onion soup in bowl, stir and mix well. Pour over chicken.
- Cover and cook on low for 5 to 6 hours if chicken breasts are large, 3 to 4 hours if breasts are medium. Serves 6.

TIP: Serve chicken and sauce with hot rice or mashed potatoes.

Perfect Chicken Breasts

6 small boneless, skinless chicken breast halves
6 slices bacon
2 280-g (10-ounce) cans mushroom soup
½ teaspoon beef stock powder

- Roll each chicken breast with slice of bacon and secure with toothpick. Place in slow cooker, overlapping as little as possible.
- Combine mushroom soup, stock powder and ½ cup (125 ml) water or milk in saucepan, heat just enough to mix well and spoon over chicken breasts.
- Cover and cook on low for 6 to 8 hours. Serves 6.

TIP: When cooked, you will have a great 'gravy' that is wonderful served over noodles or rice.

Island Chicken

250 ml (8 ounces) Thousand Island salad dressing
450 g (16 ounces) whole-berry cranberry sauce
1 30-g (1-ounce) packet onion soup mix
1 whole chicken, skinned and quartered
Rice, cooked

- Combine dressing, cranberry sauce, ½ cup (125 ml) water and soup mix in bowl. Stir well. Place chicken pieces in 6-L (6-quart) oval slow cooker and spoon dressing-cranberry mixture over chicken.
- Cover and cook on low for 4 to 5 hours. Serve sauce and chicken over rice. Serves 4 to 6.

TIP: If you don't want to cut up a chicken, use 6 chicken breasts.

Chicken Fettuccini

5–6 boneless, skinless chicken breast halves
1 teaspoon chicken seasoning
1 280-g (10-ounce) can cream of chicken soup
1 280-g (10-ounce) can cream of celery soup
100 g (3½ ounces) cheddar cheese, shredded
½ cup (125 ml) white cooking wine
1 340-g (12-ounce) package fettuccini (medium noodles), cooked

- Cut chicken breasts in half if they are unusually large. Place breast halves, sprinkled with pepper and chicken seasoning, in sprayed slow cooker.
- Combine soups, cheese and wine in saucepan and heat enough to mix well and melt cheese. Pour over chicken.
- Cover and cook on low for 5 to 6 hours. Serve chicken and sauce over pasta. Serves 6.

Saffron Rice and Chicken

1 whole chicken, quartered
½ teaspoon garlic powder
Olive oil
400 ml (14 ounces) chicken stock
1 onion, chopped
1 green capsicum, seeded and chopped
1 yellow capsicum, seeded and chopped
1 115-g (4-ounce) jar roasted red capsicum, drained
⅓ cup (40 g) bacon bits
1 145-g (5-ounce) package saffron rice mix
2 tablespoons (30 g) butter, melted

- Sprinkle chicken with garlic powder and a little salt and pepper. Brown chicken quarters in frypan with a little oil. Place chicken in sprayed slow cooker and pour stock into slow cooker.
- Combine onion, capsicums, roasted red capsicum and bacon bits in bowl and spoon over chicken quarters. Cover and cook on low for 4 to 5 hours.
- Carefully remove chicken quarters from cooker, stir in rice mix and butter and return chicken to cooker. Cover and cook for 1 hour or until rice is tender. Serves 4 to 6.

Savoury Chicken Fettuccini

900 g (2 pounds) boneless, skinless chicken thighs, cubed
½ teaspoon garlic powder
1 red capsicum, seeded and chopped
2 sticks celery, chopped
1 280-g (10-ounce) can cream of celery soup
1 280-g (10-ounce) can cream of chicken soup
230 g (8 ounces) cubed processed cheese
1 115-g (4-ounce) jar diced roasted red capsicum
450 g (16 ounces) spinach fettuccini

- Place chicken in sprayed slow cooker. Sprinkle with garlic powder, ½ teaspoon pepper, capsicum and celery. Mix soups (do not add water) in bowl and pour on chicken.
- Cover and cook on high for 4 to 6 hours or until chicken juices are clear. Stir in cheese and roasted red capsicum. Cover and cook until cheese melts.
- Cook pasta according to package directions and drain. Place fettuccini in serving bowl and spoon chicken over fettuccini. Serve hot.

Slow-Cooked Arroz con Pollo

This is a classic Mexican chicken and rice dinner, but cooked conveniently in a slow cooker.

3–4 pounds boneless, skinless chicken breasts and thighs
1 425-g (15-ounce) can tomatoes
2 teaspoons Mexican spice mix
1½ cups (280 g) long grain rice
85 g (3 ounces) yellow rice mix with seasoning
800 ml (27 ounces) chicken stock
1 clove garlic, minced
1 teaspoon oregano

- Combine all ingredients plus ¾ cup (175 ml) water in large, sprayed slow cooker and stir well.
- Cover and cook on low for 7 to 8 hours or on high for 3 hours 30 minutes to 4 hours. Serves 10 to 12.

Slow-Cooker Cordon Bleu

4 boneless, skinless chicken breast halves
4 slices cooked ham
4 slices Swiss cheese, softened
1 280-g (10-ounce) can cream of chicken soup
¼ cup (60 ml) milk
Pasta, cooked

- Place chicken breasts on cutting board and pound until breast halves are thin. Place ham and cheese slices on chicken breasts, roll and secure with toothpick.
- Arrange chicken rolls in 4-L (4-quart) slow cooker. Thin chicken soup with milk in saucepan, heat just enough to mix well and pour over chicken rolls.
- Cover and cook on low for 4 to 5 hours. Serve over pasta and cover with sauce from soup. Serves 4.

Slow-Cooked Chicken Fajitas

This is a convenient way to have a popular one-pot dinner.

900 g (2 pounds) boneless, skinless chicken breast halves
1 onion, thinly sliced
1 red capsicum, seeded and sliced
1 teaspoon ground cumin
1½ teaspoons chilli powder
1 tablespoon (15 ml) lime juice
½ cup (125 ml) chicken stock
8–10 warmed flour tortillas
Guacamole
Sour cream
Lettuce
Tomatoes

- Cut chicken into diagonal strips and place in sprayed slow cooker. Top with onion and capsicum.
- Combine cumin, chilli powder, lime juice and chicken stock in bowl and pour over chicken and vegetables. Cover and cook on low for 5 to 7 hours.
- When serving, spoon several slices of chicken mixture with sauce into centre of each warm tortilla and fold. Serve with guacamole, sour cream, lettuce and/or tomatoes. Serves 8.

Chicken Little Slow-Cook

4 boneless, skinless chicken breast halves
1 280-g (10-ounce) can French onion soup
2 teaspoons chicken seasoning
1 115-g (4-ounce) jar sliced mushrooms, drained
1 cup (115 g) shredded mozzarella cheese

- Brown each chicken breast in frypan and place in slow cooker.
- Pour onion soup over chicken and sprinkle pepper and chicken seasoning over chicken breasts.
- Place mushrooms and cheese over chicken breasts. Cover and cook on low for 4 to 5 hours. Serves 4.

TIP: *To make this chicken extra-tasty when ready to serve, sprinkle some chopped spring onions over each serving.*

The term 'feathered out' is used when a chick loses its baby fluff and grows its feathers.

So-Good Chicken

4–5 boneless, skinless chicken breast halves
1 280-g (10-ounce) can mushroom soup
1 cup (250 ml) white cooking wine
230 g (8 ounces) sour cream

- Wash chicken and dry with paper towels. Sprinkle a little salt and pepper over each breast and place in slow cooker.
- Combine mushroom soup, wine and sour cream in saucepan and heat just enough to mix well. Spoon over chicken breasts. Cover and cook on low for 5 to 7 hours. Serves 5.

Lemon Chicken

1.1–1.4 kg (2½–3 pounds) chicken, quartered
1 teaspoon dried oregano
2 teaspoons minced garlic
2 tablespoons (30 g) butter
¼ cup (60 ml) lemon juice

- Season chicken with salt, pepper and oregano and rub garlic on chicken.
- Brown chicken on all sides in butter in frypan and transfer to sprayed slow cooker.
- Add ⅓ cup (75 ml) water to frypan, scrape bottom and pour over chicken.
- Cover and cook on low for 5 to 7 hours.
- Pour lemon juice over chicken and cook for an additional 1 hour. Serves 6.

Southern Chicken

1 cup (250 ml) light cream
1 tablespoon (15 g) flour
1 30-g (1-ounce) packet chicken gravy mix
450 g (1 pound) boneless, skinless chicken thighs
450 g (16 ounces) frozen stew vegetables, thawed
1 115-g (4-ounce) jar sliced mushrooms, drained
280 g (10 ounces) frozen green peas, thawed
1½ cups (180 g) scone mix
1 bunch spring onions, chopped
½ cup (125 ml) milk

- Combine cream, flour, gravy mix and 1 cup (250 ml) water in bowl, stir until smooth and pour into large slow cooker.
- Cut chicken into 2.5-cm (1-inch) pieces and add to slow cooker. Stir in stew vegetables and mushrooms.
- Cover and cook on low for 4 to 6 hours or until chicken is tender and sauce thickens. Stir in peas.
- Combine scone mix, spring onions and milk in bowl and mix well. Drop tablespoonfuls of dough onto chicken mixture.
- Change heat to high, cover and cook for an additional 50 to 60 minutes. Serves 8.

Southwestern Chicken Pot

6 boneless, skinless chicken breast halves
1 teaspoon ground cumin
1 teaspoon chilli powder
1 280-g (10-ounce) can cream of chicken soup
200 g (7 ounces) processed cheese spread
1½ cups (400 g) salsa
Rice, cooked
Flour tortillas

- Place chicken breasts in sprayed slow cooker sprinkled with cumin, chilli powder and some salt and pepper.
- Combine soup, cheese spread and salsa in saucepan. Heat just enough to mix and pour over chicken breasts.
- Cover and cook on low for 6 to 7 hours. Serve over rice with warmed flour tortillas. Serves 6.

Sweet-and-Spicy Chicken

900 g (2 pounds) chicken thighs
¾ cup (200 g) chilli sauce
¾ cup (165 g) packed brown sugar
1 30-g (1-ounce) packet onion soup mix
⅛ teaspoon cayenne pepper
Rice, cooked

- Arrange chicken pieces in bottom of sprayed 5-L (5-quart) slow cooker.
- Combine chilli sauce, brown sugar, onion soup mix, cayenne pepper and ¼ cup (60 ml) water in bowl and spoon over chicken.
- Cover and cook on low for 6 to 7 hours. Serve over rice. Serves 6.

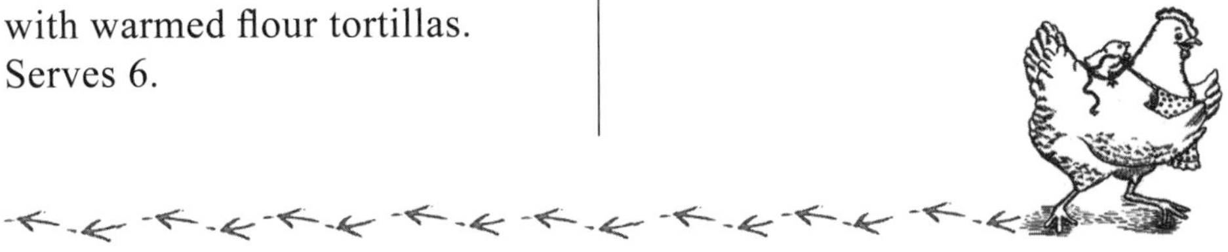

Slow-Cooked Taco Chicken

3 cups (420 g) cooked, chopped chicken
1 30-g (1-ounce) packet taco seasoning
1 cup (185 g) white rice
2 cups (200 g) chopped celery
1 green capsicum, seeded and chopped
2 425-g (15-ounce) cans tomatoes
2 teaspoons Mexican spice mix

- Combine chicken, taco seasoning, rice, celery, capsicum, tomatoes and spice mix in bowl and mix well.
- Pour into 5-L (5-quart) slow cooker. Cover and cook on low for 3 to 4 hours. Serves 8.

TIP: This is a great recipe for leftover chicken.

Tangy Chicken Legs

12–15 chicken legs
⅓ cup (75 ml) soy sauce
⅔ cup (150 g) packed brown sugar
⅛ teaspoon ground ginger

- Place chicken legs in 5-L (5-quart) slow cooker.
- Combine soy sauce, brown sugar, ¼ cup (60 ml) water and ginger in bowl and spoon over chicken legs.
- Cover and cook on low for 4 to 5 hours. Serves 6.

Tasty Chicken with Rice and Veggies

4 boneless, skinless chicken breast halves
560 g (20 ounces) sweet-and-sour sauce
450 g (16 ounces) frozen broccoli florets, cauliflower and carrots, thawed
280 g (10 ounces) frozen baby peas, thawed
2 cups (200 g) sliced celery
170 g (6 ounces) instant rice
60 g (2 ounces) parmesan cheese, grated
⅓ cup (55 g) slivered almonds, toasted
Rice, cooked

- Cut chicken into 2-cm (1-inch) strips.
- Combine chicken, sweet-and-sour sauce and all vegetables in 6-L (6-quart) sprayed slow cooker. Cover and cook on low for 4 to 6 hours.
- When ready to serve cook rice according to package directions and fold in parmesan and almonds.
- Serve chicken and vegetables over rice. Serves 4.

Tortilla Flats Chicken Bake

6 15-cm (6-inch) corn tortillas
3 cups (420 g) cooked, cubed chicken
280 g (10 ounces) frozen corn
1 425-g (15-ounce) can borlotti beans with juice
450 g (16 ounces) hot salsa
¼ cup (60 g) sour cream
1 tablespoon (15 g) flour
3 tablespoons (30 g) chopped fresh coriander
230 g (8 ounces) shredded cheddar blend

- Cut tortillas into 6 wedges. Place half of tortilla wedges in sprayed slow cooker.
- Layer chicken, corn and beans over tortillas in slow cooker.
- Combine salsa, sour cream, flour and coriander in bowl and pour over corn and beans. Cover and cook on low for 3 to 4 hours.
- Place remaining tortilla wedges on baking tray, bake for about 10 minutes at 120° C (250° F) and set aside.
- When ready to serve, place baked tortilla wedges and cheese on top of each serving. Serves 6.

Tom Turkey Bake

680 g (1½ pounds) turkey tenderloins
1 170-g (6-ounce) package Oriental-flavoured instant rice
280 g (10 ounces) frozen green peas, thawed
1 cup (100 g) sliced celery
¼ cup (60 g) butter, melted
400 ml (14 ounces) chicken stock
1½ cups (105 g) fresh broccoli florets

- Cut tenderloins into strips. Sauté turkey strips in non-stick frypan until no longer pink.
- Combine turkey strips, rice with seasoning packet, peas, celery, butter, chicken stock and 1 cup (250 ml) water in large slow cooker and mix well.
- Cover and cook on low for 4 to 5 hours. Turn heat to high setting, add broccoli and cook for an additional 20 minutes. Serves 6.

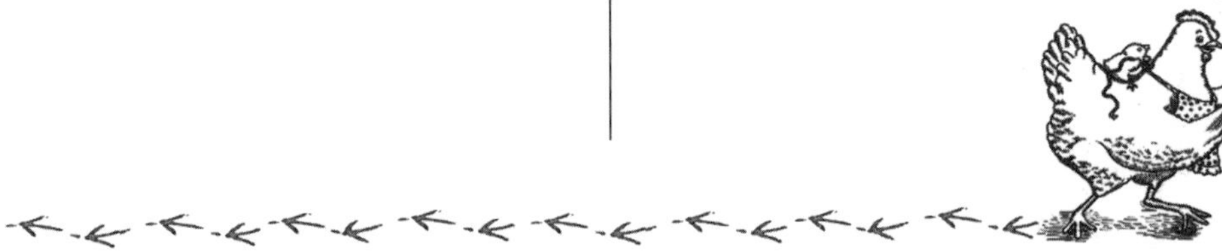

Turkey and Chicken Sausage Simmer

This is a great recipe for leftover turkey.

2 cups (280 g) cooked, cubed turkey
230 g (½ pound) chicken sausages, cooked
3 carrots, sliced
1 onion, halved and sliced
1 425-g (15-ounce) can cannellini beans
1 425-g (15-ounce) can white butter beans
230 g (8 ounces) tomato simmer sauce
1 teaspoon dried thyme
¼ teaspoon ground allspice

- Cut chicken sausages in 1-cm (½-inch) pieces. Combine all ingredients in sprayed slow cooker. Cover and cook on low for 4 to 5 hours. Serves 6.

Gobble-It-Up Turkey Loaf

900 g (2 pounds) minced turkey
1 onion, very finely chopped
½ red capsicum, seeded and very finely chopped
2 teaspoons minced garlic
½ cup (135 g) chilli sauce
2 large eggs, beaten
¾ cup (90 g) Italian seasoned breadcrumbs
Salsa

- Combine all ingredients plus 1 teaspoon salt and ½ teaspoon pepper in large bowl and mix well. Shape into round loaf and place in slow cooker.
- Cover and cook on low for 5 to 6 hours. Remove from cooker to serving plate and serve with salsa. Serves 8.

Chicken Sausage and Rice

450 g (1 pound) chicken sausage
170 g (6 ounces) chicken-flavoured instant rice
800 ml (27 ounces) chicken stock
2 cups (200 g) sliced celery
1 red capsicum, julienned
1 425-g (15-ounce) can sliced green beans, drained
⅓ cup (55 g) slivered almonds, toasted

- Break up chicken sausages and brown in frypan. Place in sprayed 4 to 5-L (4 to 5-quart) slow cooker. Add rice, 1 cup (250 ml) water, chicken stock, celery, capsicum and green beans and stir to mix.
- Cover and cook on low for 3 to 4 hours. When ready to serve, sprinkle almonds over top. Serves 8.

Tomato Chicken Spaghetti

900 g (2 pounds) minced chicken
2 280-g (10-ounce) cans tomato soup
400 ml (14 ounces) chicken stock
1 425-g (15-ounce) can corn, drained
1 115-g (4-ounce) jar sliced mushrooms, drained
¼ cup (70 g) tomato sauce
400 g (14 ounces) spaghetti

- Cook chicken mince in non-stick frypan and season with a little salt and pepper. Place cooked chicken in sprayed 5 to 6-L (5 to 6-quart) slow cooker.
- Combine soup, stock, corn, mushrooms and ketchup in bowl and stir to blend. Add spaghetti to slow cooker and pour soup mixture on top. Cover and cook on low for 5 to 7 hours or on high for 3 hours. Serves 8.

Winter Dinner

450 g (1 pound) chicken tenderloins
Olive oil
450 g (1 pound) Polish sausage
2 onions, chopped
2 400-g (14-ounce) cans borlotti beans
1 425-g (15-ounce) can Mexican-style beans, drained
1 425-g (15-ounce) can butter beans, drained
1 cup (270 g) tomato sauce
1 cup (220 g) packed brown sugar
1 tablespoon (15 ml) vinegar
6 slices bacon, cooked and crumbled

- Brown chicken slices in frypan with a little oil and place in large sprayed slow cooker.
- Cut sausage into 2-cm (1-inch) pieces and add to slow cooker.
- Combine onions, beans, tomato sauce, brown sugar and vinegar in bowl, add to slow cooker and stir gently.
- Cover and cook on low for 7 to 8 hours or on high for 3 hours 30 minutes to 4 hours. When ready to serve, sprinkle crumbled bacon over top. Serves 12.

The town of Chicken in Alaska got its name because the locals wanted to honour the state bird, the ptarmigan, by naming their town Ptarmigan, Alaska. Unfortunately, they couldn't spell ptarmigan. However, they could spell chicken.

One Last Peep

Ingredient Equivalents

Convenience Foods to Keep on Hand

Index

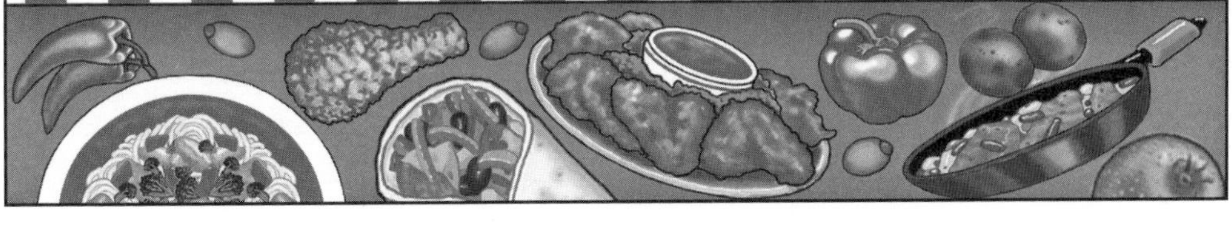

Ingredient Equivalents

Food	Amount	Approximate Equivalent
Apples	450 g (1 pound) fresh	3 medium 2¼ cups chopped 3 cups sliced
Bacon	1 slice, cooked	1 tablespoon crumbled
Bread	450 g (1 pound) loaf	14–18 regular slices 7 cups crumbs
	1 slice	½ cup crumbs
Breadcrumbs	230 g (8 ounces)	2⅓ cups
Breadcrumbs, dry	1 cup	¾ cup cracker crumbs
Broccoli	450 g (1 pound) fresh	2 cups chopped
Stock, chicken or beef	1 cup	1 stock cube 1 teaspoon stock powder in 1 cup boiling water
Butter	450 g (1 pound)	2 cups
	125 g (4½ ounces)	½ cup 8 tablespoons
	1 cup (8 ounces)	⅞ cup vegetable oil or shortening 1 cup margarine
Buttermilk	1 cup	1 tablespoon lemon juice or white vinegar plus milk to equal 1 cup (must stand for 10 minutes)
Capsicums	2 large	2½ cups chopped 3 cups sliced
	1 medium	1 cup chopped
Celery	2 sticks	½ cup chopped
Chicken	1.4–1.6 kg (3–3½ pounds)	3 cups cooked meat
	1 whole breast	1½ cups cooked and chopped

Food	Amount	Approximate Equivalent
Chocolate	170 g (6 ounces) chips	1 cup
Chocolate biscuits	18–20 biscuits	1 cup crumbs
Cornflour	1 tablespoon	2 tablespoons flour
Cottage cheese	1 cup	1 cup ricotta
Cream	250 ml (½ pint) light	1 cup
	250 ml (½ pint) whipping	1 cup; 2 cups whipped
	250 ml (½ pint) sour cream	1 cup
Cream cheese	250 g (8 ounces)	1 cup
Flour	1 cup sifted plain	1 cup minus 2 tablespoons unsifted plain
	1 cup sifted self-raising	1 cup sifted plain flour plus 1½ teaspoons baking powder plus ⅛ teaspoon salt
Garlic	1 small clove	⅛ teaspoon garlic powder
Ham	230 g (½ pound) boneless	1½ cups chopped
Herbs	1 tablespoon fresh	1 teaspoon dried
Honey	1 cup	1¼ cups granulated sugar plus ⅓ cup liquid in recipe
Lemon juice	1 teaspoon	½ teaspoon vinegar
Lemons	4–6	1 cup juice
Limes	6–8	¾ cup juice
Macaroni	230 g (8 ounces)	4 cups cooked
	1 cup	1¾ cups cooked
Marshmallows	6–7 large	1 cup
	85 miniature	1 cup
Milk	1 L (1 quart)	4 cups
Milk, evaporated	150 g (5 ounces)	⅔ cup

Food	Amount	Approximate Equivalent
Mushrooms	230 g (½ pound) fresh	1 170 g (6 ounce) can, drained
	450 g (1 pound)	5 cups sliced; 6 cups chopped
Mustard	1 tablespoon prepared	1 teaspoon dry
Oil	1 L (1 quart)	4 cups
Onions	1 small	1 tablespoon instant minced ½ tablespoon onion powder
Onions, spring	5 bulbs only	½ cup chopped
	5 with tops	1¾ cups chopped
Onions, white	4 medium	3½ cups chopped
Peaches	4 medium	2½ cups chopped or sliced
Peanut butter	500 g (18 ounce) jar	1¾ cups
Pecans	450 g (1 pound) shelled	4 cups chopped
Potatoes, sweet	3 medium	4 cups chopped
Potatoes, white, red, russet	450 g (1 pound)	4 cups chopped
Prawns	450 g (1 pound) shelled	2 cups cooked
	450 g (1 pound) in shell	20–30 large 11–15 jumbo
Rice	1 cup white	3 cups cooked
	1 cup instant	2 cups cooked
	1 cup brown	4 cups cooked
	1 cup wild	4 cups cooked
Shortening	450 g (1 pound)	2½ cups
Sour cream	1 cup	1 cup plain yoghurt ¾ cup buttermilk 1 tablespoon lemon juice plus enough evaporated milk to equal 1 cup
Squash, yellow	450 g (1 pound)	3 cups sliced

Food	Amount	Approximate Equivalent
Strawberries	350 g (1 pint) fresh	1½ cups sliced
	280 g (10 ounces) frozen	1½ cups
Sugar	1 cup light brown	½ cup packed brown sugar plus ½ cup granulated sugar
	1 cup granulated	1¾ cups icing sugar 1 cup packed brown sugar 1 cup caster sugar
	450 g (1 pound) granulated	2 cups
	450 g (1 pound) icing	3½ cups
	450 g (1 pound) brown	2¼ cups packed
Tomatoes	3 medium	1½ cups chopped
Tomato juice	1 cup	½ cup tomato paste plus ½ cup water
Tomato sauce	½ cup	½ cup tomato sauce plus 2 tablespoons sugar plus 1 tablespoon vinegar
Vanilla biscuits	22 biscuits	1 cup crumbs
Wine	750 ml (1½ pints)	3 cups
Yoghurt	1 cup	1 cup buttermilk 1 cup milk plus 1 tablespoon lemon juice

Convenience Foods to Keep on Hand

Canned Savoury Foods

- Whole and chopped tomatoes
- Beans
- Vegetables such as corn, asparagus, and artichoke hearts
- Tuna
- Cooked ham
- Sauces
- Condensed and ready-to-heat soups
- Peanut and other nut butters
- Ready-made meals such as chilli or baked beans

Canned Sweet Foods

- Pineapple
- Pear rings and chunks
- Peach halves or slices
- Exotic fruits such as lychees and guavas
- Fruit pie fillings
- Apple sauce
- Fruit salad

Dry Foods and Packaged Mixes

- Sauce and gravy mixes
- Dried vegetables and beans
- Instant mashed potatoes
- Pasta
- Rice and rice mixes
- Instant desserts
- Dried milk
- Gelatine
- Bread
- Pastry
- Cake mixes
- Bottled foods and preserves
- Jams and jellies
- Pesto
- Olives
- Sun-dried tomatoes
- Antipasto

Prepared Foods

- Partly baked breads and pastries
- Prepared ready-to-serve meals
- Boil-in-the-bag rice
- Desserts

Refrigerated Foods

- Milk and cream
- Prepared meals
- Fresh pasta
- Soups
- Sweet and savoury sauces
- Fruit salad
- Bag salads and dressings
- Fresh pastry
- Dips
- Eggs

Frozen Savoury Foods

- Vegetables and stir-fry mixes
- Chips
- Cooked rice
- Pizza bases
- Prepared fish and shellfish
- Meat and poultry

Frozen Sweet Foods

- Fruits and seasonal soft-fruit mixes
- Melon balls
- Ice-creams, sorbets, and iced desserts
- Pastry
- Pies
- Cakes
- Fruit juices

Index

A

B

Casseroles

D

E

F

G

H

I

J

K

L

M

N

O

P

Q

R

S

T

V

W

Y

Z